metro

MITCHELL BEAZLEY

metro

the story of the underground railway **david bennett**

Metro

David Bennett

First published in Great Britain in 2004 by Mitchell Beazley,
an imprint of Octopus Publishing Group Ltd
2–4 Heron Quays, London E14 4JP

ISBN 1 84000838 5

A CIP catalogue copy of this book is available
from the British Library

Commissioning Editor: Hannah Barnes-Murphy

Executive Art Editor: Sarah Rock

Senior Editor: Peter Taylor

Design: Hoop Design

Production: Gary Hayes

To order this book as a gift or incentive, contact
Mitchell Beazley on 020 7531 8481

Title page image: Hostafrancs Station, Barcelona

Set in Joanna and Akzidenz Grotesk

Produced by Toppan Printing Co. (HK) Ltd
Printed and bound in China

contents

foreword

right **Paris did not have the first metro in the world, but it is perhaps the best known, due in part to the iconic Art Nouveau entrances created by Hector Guimard.**

In most major cities in the world today there is a metro – an underground railway – just as there are buildings, roads, cars, sewers, and street lighting. As the city has grown, so its building density has dramatically increased. Many of our streets and roadways were built more than a hundred years ago, primarily for carrying slow-moving, horse-drawn carriages, hand-pulled carts, and the first automobiles. They are now too narrow to cope with the volume of traffic generated by today's commuters, shoppers, tourists, and city-dwellers. Smog, pollution, and traffic jams have become a feature of many modern cities. However, for a city to grow, and in order to keep its business heart alive, it must provide the means for people to move from place to place quickly. There is now international consensus that there is only one way to solve traffic congestion in cities: by the construction of underground transport corridors.

Without the underground or subway network, a modern city would simply grind to a halt. It is no longer the car, but the train that keeps the city alive. For nearly a hundred years the design of trains, the construction of the tunnels, the methods of digging below ground, the locomotive power to drive trains, and the distances travelled have been continually extended, upgraded, improved, and modernized to keep pace with urban growth. In 1840 the first modern tunnel was excavated under the River Thames in

London, from Wapping to Rotherhithe, to alleviate congestion on London Bridge. In 1820 the bridge was grid-locked with more than 400 hand-carts and horse-drawn wagons crossing daily to make a four-mile journey from the docks on the north side to the mills and factories on the south bank, and back again. It took nearly 15 years to excavate and complete the Thames Tunnel; a distance of only 400m (1,300ft). Marc Isambard Brunel's extraordinary tunnelling shield was operated by labourers who would hand dig the soil from within an iron framework at the rate of 30cm (12in) per day. Today a modern tunnelling machine, such as that used on the Jubilee Line Extension in London, could have completed the Thames Tunnel in just 30 days – a measure of how far technology in tunnelling has advanced.

Unfortunately, just when we think the world is a better place for the underground, we are reminded of the overcrowding, the poor service, and regular breakdowns of the underground railway in cities where it has been in

below **Chicago's metro is nicknamed the "El" as most of its network is elevated. Some stretches of the present system date back to the end of the 19th century.**

metro

operation for more than a hundred years. The original tunnel size, the station platform lengths, and train intervals are unable to cope with the demands of commuter traffic today. New into old won't work anymore without drastic overhaul and a bottomless pit of money. With cities becoming saturated with train tunnels, there is an increasing risk that further tunnelling will undermine building foundations and existing tunnels and cause collapses. Way back in the 1950s, the French engineers were very forward-thinking in converting all the Paris Métro trains to rubber-wheeled ones to ensure they could increase the line capacity without having to widen the tunnels or lengthen the platforms. To alleviate congestion in the underground today, elevated light railways, trams, and trolley buses are being re-introduced into our streets. Congestion problems have come full circle.

But the aim of this book has been to go beyond purely telling the story of the metro as a history lesson about the building of tunnels and the early underground railways of London, Boston, and Paris. Rather, it provides an insight into underground travel the world over, from the early coal-burning locomotives to the electrification of the line, explaining why some trains run on rubber wheels and not on steel ones, exploring the changing trends in

above **Tunnelling work in progress on the extension to Jubilee Line in south-east London. Work began in 1993 and was completed six years later.**

right, top **A Paris Métro train crosses the Seine on the Austerlitz viaduct. In the early years of the Métro it was felt that the tunnelling technology was insufficiently advanced to tunnel under the river.**

right, bottom **The Istanbul metro near 4 Levent station. The system was specially constructed to withstand earthquakes.**

metro station design and the introduction of art and sculpture to make the daily subterranean journey a delight. It also takes a look at poster and graffiti art, the evolution of the subway map, and escalator design.

I am indebted to so many people and metro organizations that have helped to make this book possible. Not in any order of importance nor weight of contribution, these are the individuals who have been my champions: Richard Lewis on tunnelling; Joanna Canton at Atlas Copco; Elaine West at Alstom; Christianne Kim Chueng Lam in Hong Kong; Andrew Mead and Marianne Hussain in Singapore; Larry Levine in Washington; Helen Lessick and Ed Scannell in Los Angeles; Claude Carrau and Philippe Benoit in Paris; Lynn Matis in Boston; Christina Malaugh and Marilyn Bolton in Toronto; Peter Verbruggen and Ingrid Andre in Brussels; Eva-Britt Gullers in Stockholm; Paul Kramer in Munich; Detlef Kramme in Berlin and Brian White at Kone (UK). Special mention must go to Hugh Robertson of the London Transport Museum and to Michael Chrimes and Rob Thomas at the Institution of Civil Engineers in London for their painstaking book and picture research on the early history of the metro. Thanks also to Chris Atkinson and Jenny Faithful for their help with translations, to Peter Taylor at Mitchell Beazley for his sterling editing skill and diligent picture collation, and to Hannah Barnes-Murphy at Mitchell Beazley, who believed that this book was worth publishing.

David Bennett, May 2004

the rise of
the metro

MISERIES OF LONDON.

In going out to dinner (already too late) your carriage delayed by a jam of coaches — which choak up the whole street. and allow you at least an hour or more than you require. to sharpen your wits for table talk ——

" Breast against breast with ruinous afsault
" And deafning shock. they come ——

Pub.d Feb.y 1.st 1807 by R Ackerman N.o 101 Strand

early tunnelling
pioneers

The rapid development of London as a port and the building of secure, high-walled enclosed docks just after the turn of 19th century made the city the largest and most advanced centre for shipping in Europe. But as hundreds of masted merchant ships inched their way towards London and its vast 800-berth mooring facility, it was not uncommon to find more than 1,000 vessels log-jammed in the Thames. A ship could take six weeks to reach the "legal quays" between the Tower of London and London Bridge where it would pay the cargo duty before off-loading its cargo.

Large numbers of storage warehouses were located on the south bank of the river at Rotherhithe, Bermondsey, and Greenwich, and alongside the new docks and warehouses industrial buildings emerged with their soot-blackened chimneys spewing out plumes of smoke that darkened the sky. Behind them, great

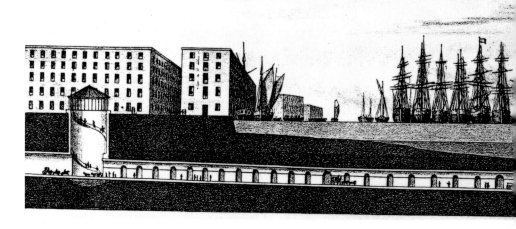

the rise of the metro

dormitory blocks of cheap housing burgeoned
for the thousands of dockworkers, navvies, and
their families who worked in the ports and
factories or on the road and rail infrastructure
that supported the shipping industry. And within
these quarters grew the poorhouses and slums of
East London, where disease was rife.

Better and easier transport access across the
river was vital. The nearest river crossing from
the docks of East London on the north to the
warehouses on the south bank was still old
London Bridge, which was becoming too
restricted and narrow to cope with the growth in
traffic. At this point on the river just as many
people were being ferried across by Thames
watermen and their boats, manoeuvring between
the hulks of slowly moving cargo ships. When
Charles Rennie's new London Bridge was opened
to road traffic in 1831 it was still too far west to
be an ideal crossing for the docklands.

This is the London that greeted Marc
Isambard Brunel when he returned to England
from New York in 1799 to make his fortune as
a civil engineer and to be reunited with his
sweetheart Sophie Kingdom. Doubtless with
his American connections and impeccable
credentials as Chief Engineer of New York, he
would have known about the need for an east
river crossing and heard the arguments for a

tunnel at Rotherhithe proposed by Vazie, a
Cornish mining engineer. The problem with a
bridge crossing was that it would need to be high
enough for ships to pass underneath. This would
cause the road ascents to be impossibly steep for
a fully laden cart and the construction cost to be
prohibitive. A bascule bridge, on the other hand,
having to remain open for a large part of the day
to allow ships to pass through, would hardly
allow a continuous flow of road traffic.

A tunnel through soft ground under a river
was a risky venture, but the concept had been
tried successfully in ancient times by the
Assyrians, when the Euphrates was diverted for a
cut and cover tunnel for the personal use of
Queen Semiramis. And the Romans were said to
have formed a tunnel under the sea at Marseilles
by heating rock then cooling it with water to split
it. For hundreds of years mining engineers had
tunnelled deep into the mountainside to reach
rich seams of coal or precious minerals. Wooden
struts, props, and headers were used to stop loose
material from falling into the excavation, which
was just large enough to take a man. But these
tunnels were dug through hard rock, which was
largely self-supporting, never intentionally
through soft water-logged ground.

Marc Brunel had read with interest the
newspaper accounts of the Vazie tunnel, which

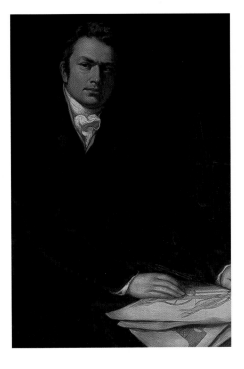

was to be built under the supervision of Cornishman Richard Trevithick and which began in 1807. After sinking the access shaft on the south bank, a driftway or small pilot tunnel was excavated, 1.5m (5ft) high and 0.9m (3ft) wide. But when the driftway had passed below the middle of the Thames and was about to rise towards the north bank, the miners encountered rock. As they chiselled through the rock they ran into quicksand, which flooded the tunnel and collapsed the unsupported roof. After clearing away the debris, pumping out the water, and making safe, they continued towards the north bank, but close to low tide mark they hit quicksand again. This time so much water poured in that the miners had to run for their lives and the directors of the Thames Archway Tunnel decided to abandoned the project.

Marc Brunel's Tunnelling Shield

The idea for a tunnel-supporting device occurred to Brunel in 1817 when he was asked by Tsar Alexander 1 of Russia to design a bridge over the River Neva at St Petersburg. Brunel thought about the possibility of forming a tunnel to reduce construction time after having studied details of Trevithick's tunnel. The project remained unbuilt, but in 1818 Brunel took out a patent for a device for "Forming Drifts and Tunnels Under Ground". It was built with a series of 12 cast-iron frames, each 0.9m (3ft) wide, 6.4m (21ft) high, and 1.5m (5ft) deep from front to back,

which were interconnected to form a tunnelling shield. The shield supported the entire roof and base of the tunnel during excavation, making it safe for the miners to tunnel through soft ground while preventing the face from collapse. It divided the face of the tunnel into 36 cells like a giant honeycomb, each one big enough for a miner to stand in and work independently of the man in the adjacent cell, allowing excavation of a tunnel face just over 70sq m (750sq ft). The area of the tunnel face in each cell was covered by horizontal "poling" boards. A miner would remove one board at a time, dig out the face to a depth of several inches, then replace the board before doing the same with the next one until he had excavated behind all the poling boards in the cell. The cell would then be pushed forward against the new tunnel face using screw jacks at the rear of the shield. Directly behind the shield followed the teams of masons and bricklayers, who lined the excavation with brick and mortar joints. Partitioning a large tunnel face into small interconnecting segments in this way enabled much wider tunnels to be dug through unstable ground, and Brunel's idea is still used today.

The route of Brunel's tunnel under the Thames ran from Rotherhithe to Wapping, linking the factories and mills on the south of the river to the wet docks of St Katherine's and West India on the north. The tunnel was constructed with two brick-lined transport carriageways within the excavation, separated by a central

left **The young Isambard Brunel using the diving bell to inspect the breach in the tunnel roof.**

below **"The Thames Tunnel Annual Grand Fete and Exhibition!" The event attracted some 66,358 people when it was first held in 1843.**

numbing regularity, largely due to the closeness of the tunnel to the silt, sewage, and rubbish that filled the bed of the Thames. There were frequent explosions in the tunnel from the sulphurated hydrogen gas released by the constant seepage of foul-smelling effluvia that poured in through the roof. It would take another 13 years before the tunnel would be ready to open to the public, by which time it was an obsolescence that had outgrown it usefulness.

Why did Brunel find the second half of the tunnelling so hazardous? His intention to excavate within the London clay below the Thames, which was impervious to water and relatively easy to dig, was sound. A careful but time-consuming test-boring along the proposed tunnel route showed that from 13m (42ft) down to 23m (76ft) below ground sound blue clay was to be found. Above this layer were loose water-bearing gravels and silts and below it the quicksand of the Woolwich Beds. The sound clay layer was only 315m (1034ft) thick and it was

arched wall to ensure a continuous flow of traffic in either direction. Work began at the Rotherhithe shaft on 2 March 1825 and was finished in nine months. It is the same shaft that you walk down when you enter Wapping underground station today.

The story of the Thames Tunnel is an epic tale of enduring courage, human tragedy, tunnel collapses, flooding disasters, and financial ruin. Within a year of completion of the Rotherhithe shaft, the tunnel excavation had reached half way under the Thames. Then disaster struck with

the rise of the metro

important that the excavation for the 6.4m (21ft) high tunnel remained within this seam, because at the deepest point of the river, the roof of the tunnel would be only 4.3m (14 ft) below the bed of the Thames. Brunel presumed that there would be an adequate depth of clay to prevent the river from pouring into the tunnel. However, it seems that as the work progressed towards the deep river bed, the depth of the clay above the tunnel roof critically reduced, particularly where the river had been dredged for gravel or navigation purposes. In places it was replaced by porous gravel, silt, and detritus that had accumulated in the river over many years.

There were many breaches in the tunnel roof and Marc Brunel's son Isambard devised a diving bell to make inspections of such breaches from the river bed. The bell was made of cast iron, weighed 3630kg (8000lb), and was lit inside by candles. The bell was lowered into the water on a chain and fed with air from a pump on the support barge. Water did not flood the bell because of the air pressure inside it, but those who sat on the seats along the wall of the bell could step into the water (or fall into it: Isambard's assistant once lost his footing and nearly perished in the mud – he was rescued by Isambard).

Two major floods, on 18 May 1827 and in January 1828, finally put an end to the project. On each occasion the large hole in the roof through which the Thames poured in had to be plugged with hundreds of tons of clay bags dropped onto the river bed by barges. Water had to be pumped out of the tunnel before the silt and mud could be carted away. It took five months to clean out the tunnel after the second flood, by which time the Thames Tunnel

company were virtually bankrupt. They decided to brick up the exposed tunnel face at mid crossing and seek more funding. There were no takers. The tunnel was left to rot for seven years before, in 1835, the Government stepped in to fund its completion. There were more tunnel collapses, more floods, more injury, more ill health, but at last, in 1841, the tunnel reached the Wapping shaft. The dual underpass and the two entrances were finished in May 1843 when the Thames Tunnel was opened to the public.

However, the carriage ramps so vital for vehicle access into the tunnel were omitted because of cash shortage. This meant that it could be used only as a pedestrian tunnel, which quickly lost its charm as thieves hid in the arches to mug passers-by. In 1869, 20 years after the tunnel opened, it was taken over by the East London Railway, which ran trains to Brighton through it. Finally the tunnel was transferred to London Underground at the turn of the century and now forms part of the Metropolitan Line.

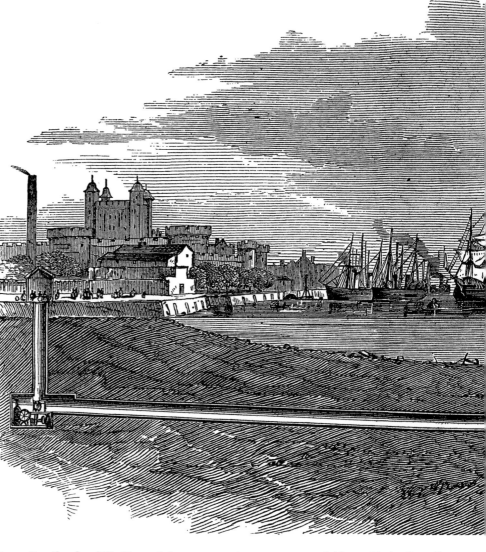

James Greathead and The Tower Subway

The second tunnel that was built under the
Thames was proposed by Peter Barlow, an
engineer who conceived of an idea for an
inexpensive yet extremely effective circular
tunnelling shield. The idea came to him while
sinking cast-iron cylinders for the piers of
Lambeth Bridge in 1863. The following year he
took out a patent for constructing tunnels by
means of cast-iron cylinders. When the contract
to build the Tower Subway tunnel for the East
London Railway company was sent out, only one
person tendered for the job; his name was James
Henry Greathead. He proposed to build the small
train tunnel from Tower Hill to Vine Lane just off
Tooley Street for just £16,000 and to complete it

in one year – remarkable considering Brunel's
tunnel cost £614,000 and took nine years to
finish. Greathead, who is regarded as the father
of modern tunnelling technology, designed and
built his own circular tunnelling shield without
apparent reference to Barlow's design and
without infringing copyright.

The front end of the Greathead shield
consisted of circular rings divided into seven
segments in which the miners worked.
Compressed air minimized the ingress of water
into the excavation and watertight bulkheads
behind the shield contained and prevented
running sands flowing into the excavation. The
shield was 2m (6ft 7in) in diameter, weighed
two and a half tons and could hold three

workmen. The tunnel lining was composed of cast-iron rings 46cm (18in) long, each ring consisting of three segments and a key-piece that rivetted together. The shield – a cylinder of cast-iron plate, slightly tapered, with the larger end at the front to reduce friction with the clay – advanced on six hydraulic rams, which pushed against the completed tunnel lining. The cavity left between the linings and the tunnel face was filled with grout inserted by hand-held syringes. The Greathead shield moved steadily forward at the rate of 2.7m (9ft) per day, completing the Tower Hill to Vine Lane tunnel in 10 months.

The bizarre and cramped underground railway that was introduced was pulled along by cable winch. It opened in 1870, carrying 12 passengers in an open-top carriage running on the single track that was laid. Unfortunately, because the carriage could only accommodate such a small volume of people, and they were only charged a penny fare for the crossing, the railway could never pay for itself and was soon forced to close. Spiral staircases were put into the 3m (10ft) diameter access shafts and the tunnel became a pedestrian subway, charging a halfpenny toll, until Tower Bridge was built in 1894. Today the tunnel carries water mains for Thames Water Authority. You can see the nondescript pillar-box entrances to the subway on Tower Hill and Vine Street.

Greathead perfected the circular tunnelling machine that still carries his name and

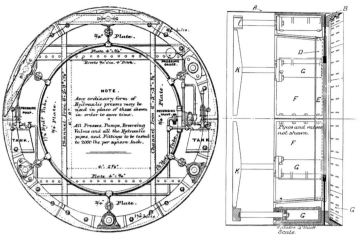

engineered the first twin-tunnelled underground railway in the world – the City and South London Line between Stockwell and London, which opened in 1890. The service ran from King William Street near the Monument, continued under the Thames south of London Bridge, past Borough High Street, and on to South Clapham to terminate in Stockwell. It was London's first deep-level tube system and the tunnels are still in service today forming part of the Northern Line, though the original tunnels have been enlarged.

In the original design the trains were to be hauled by cables with the trains running in separate tunnels, one above the other. Fortunately

for Greathead and the owners of the line, the rapid progress of electric-powered trams enabled them to switch from cable haulage to electric power before the tunnels were excavated. Greathead retained the concept of separate tunnels, arguing that two smaller tunnels were cheaper to excavate that one enormous twin tunnel; there was also less material to dispose of and greater construction safety.

The 3m (10ft) diameter tunnels were built from cast-iron rings, each ring consisting of six segments and a key-piece, and all the rivet holes were cast-in to avoid tooling of any kind to the plates. The plate and flanges were cast from soft grey pig iron and dipped into a composition of hot tar and pitch that formed a glossy black, hard-wearing coating when it cooled. The horizontal joints of the rings were packed with soft pine 6mm (¼in) thick and the vertical ones with a rope of tarred hemp to make the segments a tight fit when they were bolted together. All the joints were sealed and pointed with a cement grout, except where the tunnel was in water-bearing strata, and an iron-cement was used to caulk the joints. This was done with the compressed air in the shield turned on, which gave excellent watertight results.

Tunnelling work commenced in October 1886 with the upper tunnel driven southwards under the Thames from a temporary shaft at the Old Swan pier on the north bank of the Thames. The lower tunnel was driven under the Thames some months later, once the upper tunnel had been excavated northwards back to King William Street from the Old Swan pier and south of the Thames just beyond London Bridge station. On completion of both tunnels from King William

the rise of the metro

Street to London Bridge, 7.6m (25ft) diameter access shafts were sunk at the stations of Borough and the Elephant and Castle and the two tunnels driven northwards and southwards simultaneously to the next station points up and down the line, using four Greathead shields. This procedure continued with the other stations en-route until the tunnel reached Stockwell, with excavation averaging around 24m (80ft) a week.

The classless carriages and 2d (2 pence) flat fare attracted passengers in their thousands soon after the line opened in 1890 – despite the absence of any windows in the stuffy, cramped carriages they had to travel in. The ride was noisy and claustrophobic and earned the trains the nickname of the "padded cells". A gateman rode on the metal footplates at the end of the carriage and would call out the station names on arrival. In 1894 nearly seven million passengers were carried by the City and South London Line. The three-carriage trains were pulled by electric locomotives built by Beyer and Peacock, one of which has been preserved in the London Transport Museum.

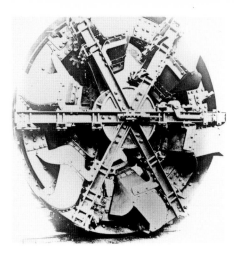

modern tunnelling techniques

Since Greathead's shield, technical advances in tunnelling haves resulted in faster and safer methods of excavation. Tunnelling through hard and soft ground are very different processes: in the former mechanical effort goes into cutting and excavating the rock; in the latter the challenge is to prevent the ground from collapsing into the excavation.

The first tunnelling machine to mechanically cut through clay soil was built by John Price in 1897 for excavating the deep-level sections of London's Central Line. Its electrically powered rotating cutter heads had four radial arms that raked back the spoil, pushing it to the middle of the machine where it dropped into chutes. The cutter head operated independently of the shield through a central drive shaft.

The Robbins machine, built some 50 years after the John Price model, evolved the design of the modern tunnelling machine. Early rock-tunnelling machines had picks that cut grooves into the rock before the disc cutter tried to split it, but it was realized that when pick heads wore away, the disc cutters still worked efficiently, creating their own grooves and splitting the rock. Double and triple disc cutters were introduced to the cutter heads until it was found that single discs positioned on a series of rotating concentric rings were more effective.

A machine built in the 1950s in England for use in soft water-logged ground conditions was known as a drum digger because the cutter head was supported on a long drum held inside the fixed outer body of the machine in order to support the excavation. The whole drum rotates on roller bearings that run along the excavation sides inside the outer drum, or shield. Thrust

bearings propel the drum and cutter head forward by pushing against the tunnel lining. The next stage in tunnelling machine development through soft ground was to support the cutter head on a single-diameter slew ring similar to that developed for hard rock excavation. This is used on most types of modern tunnelling machines. The teeth of the cutters in soft ground guide the spoil onto a conveyor belt for disposal. The drum or shield that protects the excavation is pushed forward by hydraulic rams and steers the digger. The limitation of this type of machine was that it could be used only in stable soft ground such as London Clay. In very unstable water-bearing ground, excavation still had to be carried out by hand or using pneumatic tools and compressed air was used to prevent the excavation flooding. This made tunnelling work slow and laborious.

The most far-reaching development in soft ground tunnelling was the invention of the Bentonite Tunnelling Machine patented by John Bartlett of consultants Mott Hay and Anderson and built by Robert Priestley in 1971. Bentonite is a special clay suspension, also known as Fullers Earth, which swells when it comes in contact with water and works in one of two ways. In coarse ground, such as sands and gravels, it penetrates into the strata and forms a barrier layer through which water cannot permeate. When it comes in contact with fine material like silty clays and fine sands a

membrane is created over the surface just like a sheet of polythene, allowing a supporting pressure to prevent collapse. This tunnelling machine has a slurry feed pipe that takes both the excavated spoil and bentonite to a holding tank on the surface, where they are separated. The spoil is disposed of, while the bentonite is recycled via a return pipe. In Japan, naturally occurring clays, sometimes with the addition of a polymer, may be used in place of bentonite, and the machines are known here – and elsewhere now – by their generic name of "slurry machines". Most of the development of these machines outside Japan has been carried out in Germany where the technique is known as either a Hydroshield or a Mixshield process.

One of the problems with the slurry machine is that when used in very fine silty clay soils it is very difficult to separate the slurry – bentonite or polymer – from the spoil. The Earth Pressure Balancing Machine (EPBM) was developed in Japan in 1974 to overcome this problem by combining a closed-faced slurry-type machine and with what is known as a blind shield – a Greathead shield with a bulkhead across it. A soil-conditioning chemical, which could be a polymer or a foaming agent, is injected through the bulkhead to the cutter heads and mixed in with the excavation. This action turns the excavated soil into a porridge-like consistency, which then fills the bulkhead and acts as a water sealant pressure to balance and support the unstable soil face. The material is removed by a screw conveyor at the same rate as the machine is advanced to maintain the balanced pressure. It has the advantage of avoiding the problems of pumping and cleaning large amounts of bentonite and has replaced the slurry machine in most unstable ground applications. When creating the Channel Tunnel the French engineers used EPBMs, as the ground was fissured with sandy silt on their side. Their British colleagues, on the other hand, used open face bentonite tunnelling machines because the chalk and marl on their side was was more stable.

above **A tunnel drilled from rock with concrete liners in place at Dupont Circle station on the Washington metro.**

below, left and right **Atlas Copco's hydraulically operated rock drills in action. Machines like this may be used in combination with blasting to create tunnels.**

right **The completed tunnel and track of the Sheppard Subway, Toronto. The pipe at the top of the picture is a temporary ventilation duct.**

In the early years, tunnels were always brick lined, but brick was replaced by bolted cast-iron segments because they were faster to construct. These segments were built up in rings with the extension of the tunnelling shield. As the shield moved forward, a space of about 25mm (1in) was left between the cast iron and the clay soil and this was filled by pumping in a cement and sand grout. During World War II there was a shortage of cast iron, so tunnelling engineers turned to concrete and designed precast concrete segmental linings. Initially these were bolted and flanged, a straight copy of the cast-iron lining; later more sophisticated designs were developed, with tapered profiles that slotted together like keystones. Hydraulic jacks were used to force the concrete segments into position, expanding them directly against the excavated clay without the need for grout to fill the voids except in unstable ground conditions.

Most early development work in rock tunnelling was carried out in the USA and later in Japan, Austria, and Switzerland. The excavated rock face is initially sprayed with a layer of shotcrete – a mixture of compressed air and concrete – and then lined. Although many companies have attempted with varying degrees of success to make rock-tunnelling machines, there are today only three major manufacturers: early pioneers Robbins; Wirth from Germany, who started in the 1960s; and Herrenknecht, who entered the market in the 1990s.

The New Austrian Tunnelling Method (NATM), developed in the 1970s, is a fast and efficient method for tunnelling through homogenous rock. It uses a permanent concrete lining in situ inside a rapidly constructed sprayed concrete temporary shell, which provides initial support for the rock face and allows the natural strength and arching of the rock to be utilized. It is often used in excavating short connecting tunnels, cross passages, and raking shafts to house escalators.

But not all tunnels cut through hard rock, boulders, and shale are excavated by hard rock tunnelling machines. A combination of rock drills, explosives, and rock-crunching machines is often deployed. This is an area in which the company Atlas Copco specializes, for example.

Dutch engineers have devised a unique method, called Immersed Tube Construction, of making river and canal crossings by laying completed tunnel segments in the bed of the river. Subsoil conditions of peat and clay overlying sand are ideal in this method of construction, which was used to build the Rotterdam metro under the River Mass in 1965.

Since the 1970s alignment control of tunnel machines has been carried out by laser guidance, electronic measurement, and computer calculation. The machine, driven by an experienced operator, uses electronic laser guidance to give a continuous directional signal so that small adjustments to the excavation line can be made instantaneously. Construction robots have been tried in Japan, but to date, faith in human experience has outweighed any robotic advantages.

trains and traction

In the pioneering years of the underground railway, carriages were pulled along by steam-driven engines. Acrid sulphur dioxide and soot-filled smoke stained and blackened the tunnel walls and stations as the engines belched their way around the network. The lack of adequate ventilation was a serious limitation to travel. Tunnelling engineers did not design forced ventilation systems because they assumed the movement of the train in a confined tunnel would push the air around, while in the cut and cover section it was open to the atmosphere at regular intervals. But even when smokeless, odourless electric traction replaced steam, the deep-level tubes still smelt nauseatingly of body odour, stale air, and engine fumes. Exhaust fans and forced ventilation were introduced in 1902, but it was not until conditioned, ozonized air was injected into the tunnel system in the 1920s that people accepted underground travel as a painless pleasure.

In the 1890s electricity became the clean power for running the underground railway. The great majority of the world's metros use a conductor rail, known as a third rail, to supply electricity to the motors of the metro cars. The current is picked up by special metal shoes attached to the train that slide along the conductor rail. The current rail, normally placed on the outside of the train track and carried on insulated supports, is set between 600 and 825 volts. Above ground and in open cut, the rail can ice up in cold winters. To prevent this, some metro cars, for example in Oslo and Helsinki, have spring-loaded shoes to pick up current from the underside of the third rail. This allows the top of the current rail to be insulated and protected.

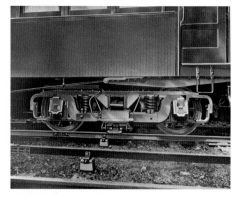

Power distribution to the current rail of any system must be carefully sectionalized so that in an emergency current can be switched off to isolate the affected area of track, leaving the rest of the system to function normally. This is usually done by positioning electrical substations to power set lengths of the track and controlling them through a central control station. Although most metro trains use current rails at track level, a number of new ones – for example in Madrid, Singapore, Hong Kong, Rome, and Japan – use overhead catenary wires. The Oedo Line of the Tokyo metro and a few other metros in Japan use linear induction motors to power their trains. Most metro trains use electricity supplied from the national grid; the two exceptions are the New York Transit and London Underground, both of which generate power from their own power stations to ensure that in a national emergency all the trains in the deep tunnels can be taken out.

The running track consists of a conventional pair of steel rails supported on either timber or precast concrete sleepers that fit into the base of the tunnel or, in open cut or when the train runs at ground level, are supported on stone ballast. The internationally adopted track gauge for the metro is 1.435m (4ft 8½in). However, many countries have different gauges, as their tracks conform to their national railway gauge. The rails are laid in 90m (300ft) lengths and welded in situ as they are laid.

Metal loss on the surface of the rails is a common problem, particularly on areas of high friction and wear, such as bends. Rust formation, caused by the damp, humid conditions in the tunnels, is another contributing factor. One of the sharpest bends for a metro system is at Bank

above **This carriage from the Berlin U–Bahn shows transverse seating, typically a feature of carriages used on long-distance journeys.**

Station on the Central Line of the London Underground. Here, and elsewhere, the rail is lubricated to reduce friction. Wear-resistant rails with one per cent chrome in the steel are specified to reduce the build up of swarfe and stop carbon being stripped from the top layers of the rail, which can lead to hair cracks and minor corrugations. But even these measures don't eliminate the problem and, to avoid the need to change the rails, which would mean closing down the system for a period, a self-propelled rail-grinding machine is used to grind the corrugations, swarfe, and rust out of the rails.

Most trains have steel wheels; the exceptions are in France, the cities of Montreal, Mexico, Santiago de Chile, and Sapporo, where they run on rubber-tyred wheels. Steel wheels support a greater load, are compatible with the steel track, and thus easy to maintain and operate, and are durable. Pneumatic rubber wheels are quieter, allow greater acceleration and braking, and increase the line capacity by travelling faster between stations, but the system requires a wide running rail and more wheels to carry the load.

The design of rolling stock is critical to the efficient operation of any underground railway carrying millions of passengers every day. There is a wide variety of rolling stock being used around the world, from the small profile cars of the Berlin U-Bahn, which are 12.6m (41ft 4in)

long and 2.35m (7ft 8in) wide, to the Hong Kong MTR whose massive carriage are 23m (75ft) long and over 3m (10ft) wide. Obviously the size of the car, the number of doors, and the ratio of seats to standing area are dictated by the number of people it has to carry at peak times and the average journey time of passengers. For example a metro that is used primarily by people taking short in-town journeys will have a small number of seats and a lot of standing room, while one that runs long distances into the suburbs will provide more seating. Where there is a low ratio of seats, these are usually arranged longitudinally along the sides of the car; where more seating is required, most will be arranged transversely.

Passenger traffic at peak and off-peak times will also dictate the frequency and number of cars per train. On relatively lightly trafficked services, a train with only two or three cars running every 10 minutes may be sufficient. Peak-time demand may require six-to-eight-car trains running at three-minute intervals. In terms of serviceability, it is highly desirable that all metro cars are identical and interchangeable, but that is never achievable if the rolling stock is a mixture of older and newer cars. Motorizing and standardizing all the stock requires a high capital investment; on the other hand, running trains with just two motorized cars and the rest trailers

the rise of the metro

below **This 1938 Central Line train from the London Underground has longitudinal seating to maximize standing room for short journeys.**

bottom **Durable, moulded plastic seating arranged longitudinally on a modern metro train in Singapore.**

is economical on capital cost but may not be best for long-term serviceability.

The bodywork and construction of the cars has echoed the development of materials through the industrial age: first wood then cast iron, steel, stainless steel, and finally lightweight aluminium. The latter greatly reduces the car weight and does not need a separate "heavy" steel chassis for the underframe, thereby reducing wear and tear on the rails. In the early days, the cars were lavishly decorated and upholstered, with carriages divided into first-, second-, and third-class compartments. As the demand for metro travel grew, the lines were extended, the frequency of trains increased, and the metro became a classless form of mass transit. Carriage interiors of necessity became more spartan and functional, hard wearing and durable. Equipment and installations have to be robust and easy to maintain to endure the punishing routine.

In planning or extending a metro line, the proportion of tunnelling to surface work and elevated construction becomes a critical factor. The high cost of tunnelling will usually limit construction to the essential minimum through congested city centre areas. The Bay Area Rapid Transit System in San Francisco has only 31km (19 miles) of tunnel; the remaining 115km (71 miles) are surface or elevated sections. Of the 392km (243 miles) of the London Underground network, only 171km (106 miles) are in tunnels. Sometimes an elevated structure can be slotted along the central reservation of a dual carriageway road or above the pavement level of streets to thread a way through the heart of built-up areas. This was done for the Kuala Lumpur and

Bangkok metros and was a considerably cheaper solution than tunnelling.

In deciding on train routes and how many branch lines to include there are a number of important factors that need to be considered. The line should follow the corridor of greatest demand and branch lines should be minimized, as too many make it difficult to bring trains together through the central section to produce a high-frequency service. Circular underground railways are generally not a good idea unless they link mainline train stations and airports: they rarely attract enough traffic to cover the capital and operating costs.

Once the preliminary route of the metro has been established, a detailed topographical and geological survey will be made to get an accurate picture of the ground level clearances, the compulsory purchase of properties that will be necessary, and the soil strata and obstructions in the ground that may be encountered. The preferred route will be one that causes least disruption and upheaval to the community and the lowest risk to the constructor.

right **Metropolitan District Line map showing the dates when sections of the line were opened.**

below **The tunnelling work was plagued by disasters, the worst of which was the bursting of the Fleet sewer and collapse of the retaining walls in June 1862.**

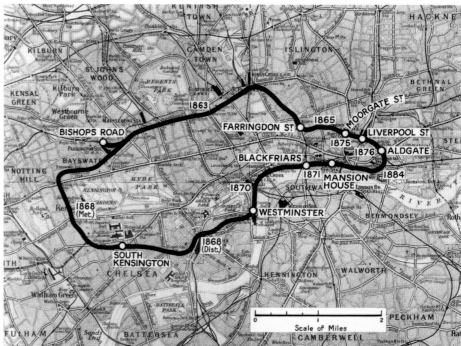

london

By the middle of 19th century, the industrial revolution, the invention of steam-powered transport, and Britain's global domination in world trade had made London the largest city in the world – and a city with the worst traffic problems. In the 1850s a quarter of a million people entered London each day to work: some came on foot, some by river steamer, others by coach or omnibus. Suburban railways already existed to take people to and from the city centre; what was needed was a transport system within the city that avoided the central thoroughfares choked with horse-drawn carts, trams, and trolley buses. Such a need gave rise to the underground railway popularly known as "the tube".

The first underground railway to be built was the Metropolitan Line, which ran a distance of 6km (3¾ miles) from Paddington to Farringdon in the heart of the business district. The story of the Metropolitan Line begins in 1843 with an idea by Charles Pearson, who was a lawyer by profession. He envisaged an underground line running beneath the surface of the road, through spacious archways that would be well ventilated and lit, from Paddington through Euston, St Pancras, and Kings Cross and on to Farringdon. It would mean the end of the squalor of the Fleet Valley slums, which would be replaced with proper housing for workers, who would have easy access to central London via the new underground railway. Pearson spent the next 14 years trying to raise the £300,000 needed to build it and in 1860 the first shaft was sunk in Euston Square.

What at first seemed a straightforward cut and cover excavation – digging deep trenches down the middle of the road, bracing the trench sides, shoring-up buildings that had shallow foundations, arching over the trench with brickwork, then rebuilding the road above it – turned into a complicated and hazardous undertaking. There were the rivers of the Fleet, Tyburn, and Westbourne to divert, together with the numerous gas pipes, water mains, and sewers that criss-crossed the excavation for its entire

left **The world's first electric railway locomotive – used on the City and South London Line – was built by Beyer and Peacock.**

below **Workmen working in a Greathead shield excavating a deep tunnel for the Northern Line around 1900.**

length. Along Euston Road the ground was largely unstable with water-bearing sands and gravels, which had to be drained and carefully supported. There were many lawsuits and claims for compensation from aggrieved property owners with cracks on their buildings or subsidence in their floors and, though not all the claims were genuine, the goodwill of the property owners was vital to maintain construction progress.

The worst disaster occurred in June 1862, when the Fleet sewer burst. The masonry walls of the railway abutments were quickly strengthened by temporary earth mounding to prevent their collapse under the increasing water pressure, but three days later the pavement in the road started to sink and the northern side of Euston Road began caving in. Suddenly the close-knit scaffolding of timber beams and struts in the trench were hurled into the air to come crashing down with a deafening roar. There were screams and shouts from thousands of onlookers, fearing for the safety of the men still in the excavation,

then an eerie silence as, slowly, the 18m (60ft) high brick piers holding back the excavation slid to the bottom of the trench. The dark fetid liquid now oozed out, submerged the brick piers, and flowed towards the mouth of the tunnel, tearing down everything in its wake and snapping massive timber piles like brittle twigs.

The Metropolitan Line eventually opened on 9 January 1863 with free rides and a grand banquet for 700 Victorian dignitaries held under a tented canopy erected in Farringdon station. Amid the celebration there was one notable absentee: Charles Pearson had died six months earlier, never to see the completion of the project that he had initiated after years of persistent lobbying, and that he had so skillfully masterminded for 20 years.

Today London Underground carries 600 million passengers a years over 1,120km (700 miles) of track that is served by 13 network lines. There are two distinct types of lines and rolling stock: the shallow cut and cover lines of the pioneering Metropolitan and Circle lines and the later District, Hammersmith and City, and East London lines, whose rolling stock are interchangeable; and the deep tunnels of the Northern, Central, Piccadilly, Victoria, Bakerloo, and Jubilee Lines, with their smaller height trains. All lines have the same track gauge though and, surprisingly, there is little difference in the carrying capacity of the trains as all are of the same width. On leaving the city centres both systems rise to the surface and continue on to the end of the line at ground level.

The first deep-level underground railway in the world, the City and South London Line, opened in 1890 and started in Stockwell. It was

the rise of the metro

built by James Greathead and is still in use today as part of the Northern Line. The Central Line, which runs east–west across London, opened in 1900 and in 1906 two lines were added to cross London diagonally: the Piccadilly Line and the Bakerloo Line. Lines were added to during the first part of the century, but after the 1940s no further extensions were considered: the underground was becoming a surface railway in the suburbs and could not support the increasing passenger numbers through the centre of its network.

The 1960s and '70s saw a rise in street congestion from traffic through central London, which resulted in the construction of two new inner-suburban underground lines: the Victoria and Jubilee Lines. The Victoria Line pioneered the use of concrete segmental linings and introduced the most successful automatic train operation system. At the interchanges, the below-ground stations were designed to give easy cross-platform transfer between lines. The Jubilee Line, which started at Charing Cross, brought commuters into the city from many suburban towns to the north-west of London. A major extension of this line has now been completed, taking the underground through two mainline railway stations south of the river and on towards the redeveloped London Docklands. The station architecture of the new Jubilee Line Extension has received world acclaim and has brought a new understanding and social awareness about the value that good architecture can bring to a city's transport infrastructure. It's a lesson that has been heeded by many other metro operators around the world.

Unfortunately, the lack of inward investment over many years, the restrictive size of the deep tunnels, and the low ceilings of the tube trains have made travel on the London Underground today – especially during the summer rush hour – a most unpleasant experience. Hopefully this is only a temporary inconvenience, as new money has been promised to rehabilitate the network.

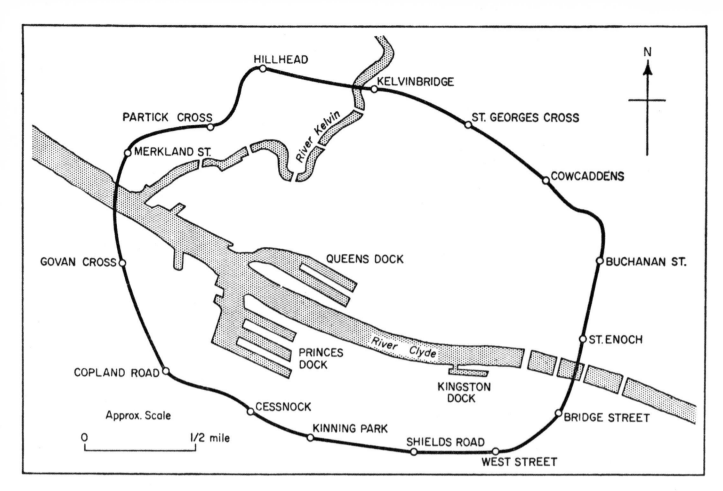

glasgow

The Glasgow Subway – or, as it affectionately known, "the clockwork orange" – is the second oldest underground railway in the world and one that never breaks the surface. It completes an oval 10.5km (6½ miles) in circumference with 15 stations and two tracks enclosed in separate tunnels with no connection between them. It was unique in many ways because the two-car trains were pulled by a moving cable positioned between the rail tracks. For the train to move the clamps that were fitted to the cars were tightened to grip the cable and for stopping the cable was released and the brakes applied. The cable was pulled along by a large cable drum powered by a 1500hp steam engine located in a large brick-built power plant. The boiler house was at the southern end of the plant and contained eight coal-fired boilers. The engine house and machinery driving the cable drums were arranged in two bays 41m (134ft) long by 15m (50ft) wide positioned side by side. Once the cables left the main engine house they entered the Tension

Run, a building 58m (190ft) long. This ensured that the cable remained at the right tension irrespective of its temperature or stretching as it aged. The cable was made up of many single strands of steel wire that were twisted together to form a rope 38mm (1½in) in diameter and was delivered to the power plant in a single length – 11km (7 miles) long – so that only one splice was required. Each cable weighed 57 tons and special transport arrangements had to be made to haul the cable drum from the factory to the plant.

Considering the cost, as well as the sheer bulk, of such an installation, it was somewhat puzzling that the Subway Company chose cable-driven cars rather than a system using electrically driven ones, such as that being proposed for the City and South London Railway and in Boston. The chief engineers and representatives of the company even went on a study trip to the USA to investigate the effectiveness of both electric- and cable-operated tramways, visiting New York, Washington, Philadelphia, Baltimore, Pittsburgh,

the rise of the metro

left **The 10.5km (6½mile) circular route of the Glasgow Metro, built in 1896.**

below **The rope drums, friction clutches, and the engine that pulled the steel cable. Each cable was 11km (7 miles) long and weighed 57 tons.**

bottom **Cars in Copland Road Station. The cable can be seen in the foreground between the rail lines.**

and Cleveland. The City and South London Railway had not yet started and it was their opinion that there was no guarantee that electrically operated trains would work underground. Moreover, cable haulage was being used successfully for trams on the streets of Glasgow and Edinburgh and would allow the underground trains to run at steeper gradients, thereby reducing construction costs.

Construction for the tunnels started at St Enoch Square in March 1881 with a shaft sunk 9.5m (31ft) below ground to the level of the tunnels. It took seven months to excavate the shaft: difficult waterlogged fine sands were encountered half way down, which slowed

the rise of the metro

progress to just a few inches a week. Fortunately, for much of their length the tunnels ran under streets, so shallow cut and cover construction was used. For the Clyde river crossing and sections under the mainline railways and away from the shallow street runs, tunnels were excavated using the Greathead shield under compressed air, and cast-iron tunnel-lining rings were installed to support the excavation. When the tunnels needed to penetrate rock and shale, dynamite was used to blast a way through.

All 15 stations on the loop had island platforms, which were raised 66cm (26in) above the rail and approached by stairs from one end. The station entrances were at street level and housed the turnstiles and pay boxes. Some entrances were constructed of red brick and built to a design by architect John Gordon, while others were built into ground floors of existing buildings. The most impressive entrance was to St Enoch station, standing on a corner of St Enoch Square. It had a façade of red Dumfriesshire stone built in the German Renaissance style, with numerous turrets, a steeply pitched roof, and a great number of dormer windows. The staircase platforms were illuminated by several pairs of 16-candle-power lamps suspended from the roof. To brighten the gloom of such dim lights the platform walls were whitewashed and lined with white tiles.

The cable-driven system worked adequately, but with such a long length of cable to pull, inevitably the cable's tensile property slackened and had to replaced – a major cost burden to the company. The passenger levels and revenue stream were never enough to make the system

economically viable. It was more labour intensive to run than the trams, especially when the trams were electrified after 1901, and the stations were dim and unattractive and did not tempt people off the trams that served the same routes. By 1922 the cable-drawn line had closed down. The Glasgow City Corporation purchased the line from the railway company and started a programme of electrification, which was completed in 1935.

Since then the underground railway has variously undergone phases of improvement and decline in passenger numbers. A three-car train was introduced in the 1950s to combat problems of overcrowding, but it was not adopted throughout the service until 1980, largely due to the high cost of replacing all the rolling stock. In the 1960s fluorescent lighting replaced tungsten lamps and the whole subway system was modernized between 1974 and 1980. This meant new rolling stock, signalling operations, gutting and relining the old tunnels, and forming a completely new concrete-based track.

In a public announcement made following the railway's refurbishment, a senior subway official said that the trains would now run like clockwork, and this remark and the coachwork's new deep-orange livery no doubt explain the adoption of the underground railway's nickname: "the clockwork orange".

left **Cut and cover excavation along Andrassy Avenue. Running the tunnel under roadways meant the work was straightforward and was able to be completed in just 20 months.**

below **A map of Budapest in 1896 showing the route of the metro.**

budapest

The earliest underground railway to be built in mainland Europe, the Budapest metro was constructed at a time when the Austro-Hungarian Empire was at it zenith and Budapest was arguably the most dynamically developed metropolis in all of Europe. (The economist Norman Macrea compared the beauty and diversity of the city's architecture and bridge-building achievements to those of Renaissance Italy.) The underground railway, which ran from Gizella Square to the City Park, traversed the length of fashionable, tree-lined Andrassy Avenue with its wooden pavements and wide vistas. The avenue was built to allow access to landaus and the omnibus, whilst prohibiting horse-drawn cabs and heavy electric trams, and was the preserve of the affluent people of the city, most of whom vehemently opposed proposals for introducing a train or tram service here.

It was six years before the dawn of the new millennium in 1894, and the city was making big plans for the celebrations, organizing a vast exhibition to be held in the City Park at one end of the avenue. The problem looming large for the organizers was how to move people quickly from one side of the city to the other without adding to the existing traffic problems on the avenue. The omnibuses were already overcrowded and the avenue was congested during day-time travel, so running more buses did not make sense. The Budapest Railway Company, who had tried unsuccessfully for many years to operate a train service along the avenue, hit on the idea of building an underground railway instead. The company was given the go-ahead on one condition: it had to be ready in time for the celebrations. The railway company promised the government that it would build the most up-to-date underground railway service in existence – one that would enhance Budapest's reputation as a world-class metropolis.

The Budapest metro still holds the record for being sanctioned in the shortest time in history – it took just five months from legislative approval

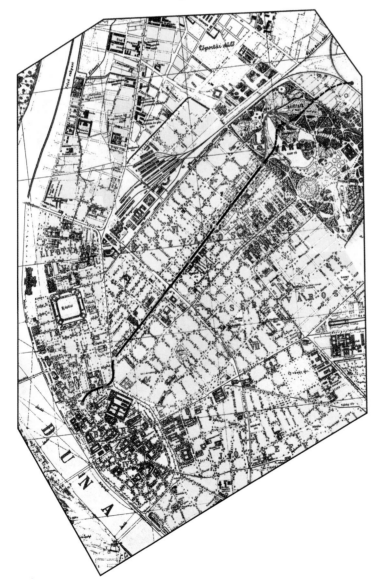

on 25 April to signing and issuing the formal document for the start on 9 August 1894 – and the underground railway itself was built and opened to the public in just 20 months. Many things helped to facilitate its speedy construction: the ground was firm and relatively easy to excavate, the tunnel was shallow and directly under the roadway with few obstructions, there were many willing hands to do the work, and there was no government interference. (Indeed, to keep up the momentum of construction the Home Secretary even approved of Sunday working.)

The most modern construction technology was used in building the tunnels, which employed electrically driven concrete mixer drums, concrete pumps, and mechanical excavators. In all 138,000m³ (180,500yds³) of excavated spoil was removed, 47,000m³ (61,500yds³) of concrete placed, and 3000 tons of cast iron forged for the structure. The footbridges that spanned the railway tracks

where the line was in open cut were the first reinforced-concrete bridges to be built in Hungary and constructed in accordance with a patented system that had been developed by Robert Wunsch.

The General Assembly of Budapest imposed an extra stipulation on the railway company: it was decreed that "special attention shall be paid from an aesthetic point of view to the ornaments of the station". The entrance canopy on street level and the staircases leading down to the platform were beautifully crafted in cast-iron latticework and tiled panels, and the staircase and walls of the station were covered in subtle patterns of brown and white glazed tiles produced by the Zsolnay china clay factory in Pecs. The cast-iron stanchion heads were decorated with splayed metalwork brackets and painted to match the soft brown of the clay tiles, and the ticket office and doorways were finished in fine hardwood frames. (The platforms themselves were covered in unattractive black

left **The distinctive canopied entrances of the Budapest metro featured delicate cast-iron lattice work.**

asphalt, but it had the advantage of being durable and hard wearing.)

The metal-clad motorized rail cars, which were ordered from the Schlick factory, were effectively tram cars adapted for an underground railway. The interiors were wood lined, slatted bench seating ran along the sides of the car, and a single sliding entry door was located in the middle of each carriage. Car number 20 was different from the others – it was the Royal carriage built for the visit of King Franz Joseph of Austria on 8 May 1896. It had polished Belgian glass windows, fine interior wood panelling, soft fabric-covered seats, and Art Nouveau-style lighting. Following the King's visit, the underground was renamed the Franz Joseph Electric Underground Railway.

During its 100 years of operation, the system has seen considerable redevelopments and improvements. The voltage of the overhead wire was increased from 330 to 550 volts, the carriages lengthened, the structure of existing tunnels strengthened, the original canopied entrances at street level removed, more sophisticated signalling equipment introduced, and the network greatly extended and modernized. In 1950 construction began of a new east–west line, which ran from the People's Stadium on the east, under the Danube, to beyond Moscow Square on the west. But with just two miles of main tunnels and 70 per cent of the running tunnels completed, work was halted in 1953, when all the labour was urgently required for the city's major post-war house-building programmes and new factory developments. Work recommenced in 1963 and Budapest now has a total underground railway

network of some 54km (34 miles) of tunnels, including the North South Metro, which runs from Upjest Kozpoint to Kobanya Kispest in the south and the line along Andrassy Avenue, which was renamed the MFAV line.

In 1995 a major restoration and redecoration programme of the original stations was undertaken, and not before time. The careworn and dilapidated stations were covered in graffiti, and a lack of regular maintenance and repairs was evident. The wall surfaces were covered in years of grime and black brake dust from the trains. New terrazzo floors in the same colour and finish as the original asphalt was laid down, the wall tiles remade to match the original in white and pale-brown patterning, new replica doors and windows installed, the cast-iron stanchions cleaned and repainted like "new" old. These stations are working, operational museum pieces and a rarity in the world of underground travel. You get a real feeling of stepping back in time to enjoy a journey from station to station that looks authentically a hundred years old.

The dilemma facing the BKV Board and their operatives today is how to plan for future improvements to the system-wide service of buses, trolley buses, and metro rail if there is a continuing risk of a drop in passenger numbers. In 1960 Budapest's inhabitants made 640 journeys per person; in 2002, for the first time in the metro's history, the steady growth in passenger numbers using public transport decreased. This was attributed to a decrease in the city population, the low price of petrol and a 14.6 per cent rise in sales of private cars that year.

below **Nagyvárad Tér
station on Line 3. This line
and Line 2 both use
conventional Soviet-made
trains, unlike the original
line (1), which requires
smaller trains because of its
different construction
method.**

bottom **Deák Square
station, the only place
where one can switch
between the three lines
on the Budapest
metro network.**

below, left **A map of the Boston tram network at the turn of the 20th century. The Tremont Street Subway, can be seen in the middle.**

bottom **This picture of Tremont Street taken on 2 June 1896 shows exactly why the Tremont Street Subway was needed – the road is clogged with trams and all other kinds of traffic. When the subway was opened three years later traffic levels were drastically reduced.**

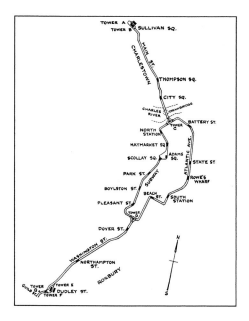

boston

Throughout the United States in the latter half of the 19th century, large cites like Washington DC, Los Angeles, and Chicago operated an extensive network of cable cars similar to the ones that still run in San Francisco today.

In Boston two cable car lines were being planned, but the management company were concerned about the high cost of construction and the running of a cable-operated system during the cold New England winters. They journeyed to Richmond, Virginia to study a new concept in tram power: the electrification of a cable- operated system. They were amazed that a small overhead copper wire could propel a tram car at such high speed.

The big question was whether the Boston tram cars could all operate on this system. An experiment was carried out by electrifying one line and parading all 22 of the company's tram cars along it. The trial was very successful, the people who came to see the parade were considerably impressed, and Boston thus became the pioneers of operating electrically driven trams, which were given the name streetcars, on a metropolitan city-wide service.

Everywhere you looked in Boston, streetcar lines were being built. Land speculators and property tycoons encouraged expansion into the more under-developed regions and watched as houses grew up around this fast and convenient mode of public transport. At one time the state of Massachusetts had more streetcar tracks per square mile than any other state in the USA. Inevitably, by the late 1880s the streets had become gridlocked. Boston's Tremont Street was so congested with streetcars that it was often quickest for passengers to walk the roof tops of the log-jammed trams to get to their destinations!

Continuous public dissatisfaction persuaded the State Government in 1891 to appoint a special commission to look into transport solutions that would reduce congestion in the streets. The territory covered by the investigation lay within 10 miles of the State House in Boston, embracing 27 towns, and supporting a population of 850,000 – a very significant number in those days. Was the answer to be an elevated light rail modelled on the success of the Chicago Loop, or an underground tramway like the one to be built

in Budapest? In April 1892 the commission recommended a solution that in fact combined both ideas: the building of four elevated tram lines and a tunnel for streetcars under Tremont Street.

On 2 July 1894 the Boston Transit Commission was incorporated with powers to plan and build subways and to determine others, and on 28 March 1895 the transit commission began construction of the Tremont Street Subway based on the concept of the Budapest tramway that ran under Andrassy Street. It started from Public Garden,

with the main subway section under Tremont Street, ran all the way to Scollay Square, and then followed the eastern side of Boston Common. From Scollay Square two northbound tracks ran onto Haymarket Square and two southbound tracks ran under Hanover Street. At Haymarket Square the track ascended to the surface, reaching level ground at Travers Street. Another section of the track branched from the corner of Boyston and Tremont Street along the southerly side of Boston Common, reaching the surface opposite Church Street.

In all the subway was 3km (nearly 2 miles) long and contained 8km (5 miles) of track. It was excavated by the cut and cover method with the roof supported on steel girder beams between which short brick vaults were built. The roof beams were propped by two rows of columns, forming portal frames, when the tunnel widened for the station platforms. By July 1897 the platforms and track under Tremont Street from Public Garden to Park Street Station was open to the public. Reporting on the opening of the subway, the *Boston Evening Record* stated: "The spaces between the seats were filled with standees; the platforms were packed like sardine boxes. Each running board was two deep with humanity, while both fenders were loaded down until there was not enough room for a fly to cling to!"

The second section, from Boylston Street to the Pleasant Street portal, opened on 7 September 1897 and less than a year later all 11 sections of the subway were complete and ready for the first through trip. The subway

entrances or kiosks were framed with an ornate canopied building with Victorian architectural ornamentation. The identical kiosks at Adams Square and Scollay Square stood in the middle of the street and featured clocks on four sides of a central tower. These buildings were replaced by simple uncovered entrances, presumably to widen the roadway. But their demise may have been accelerated by criticism from the architectural press, who thought the buildings were ugly edifices. (A reporter on one New York paper cheekily stated that they resembled mausoleums more often seen in the cemeteries of Paris!)

A later extension of the subway ran under Boston Harbour to connect with the industrial and residential suburbs of East Boston. The extension consisted of two tunnels that were 3,658m (12,000ft) long. The depth of the tunnels was mainly very shallow, but for 671m (2,200ft), they went to a deep level as they passed under Port Point Channel, which is a part of the harbour. They were constructed using tunnelling shields 7m (24ft) in diameter, weighing in at about 83 tons each.

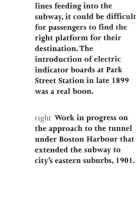

The work was carried out continuously with three eight-hour shifts over 24 hours. The maximum advance for one shield was 32m (105ft) in seven days. The average progress over nine months was 2.83m (9.3 ft) per day for the east tunnel and 3.3m (10.8 ft) per day for the west tunnel.

During the next four decades the mass transportation network in Boston and the state underwent tremendous expansion. New tram and roadway tunnels were constructed and new elevated railway lines reached out from the city into the outlying communities. One innovation pioneered by the Boston Elevated Railway was the introduction of articulated tram cars that could bend in the middle as a way to increase the tram length and make it easier to navigate the narrow streets. The Boston "El", as it was dubbed, took two 6m (20ft) streetcars and joined them together with a special articulation mechanism.

Currently, the MBTA (Massachusetts Bay Transportation Authority), who are responsible for running the Boston Metro, operate the sixth-largest mass-transit network in the USA – and that includes buses, light rail, commuter rail, trolley buses, and trams. In 1993 it served a state population of 2.6 million people covering 78 cities and towns within an area of 2,683sq km (1,036sq miles).

left **The stairs down to the subway at Adams Square station were given full-blown Victorian ornamentation by the architect Charles Brigham.**

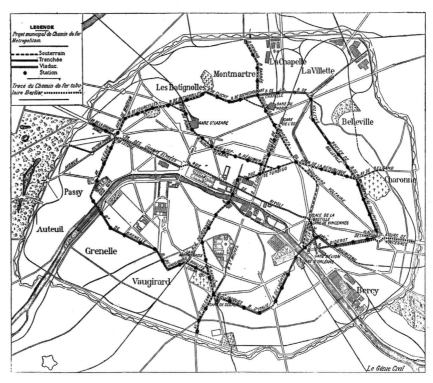

paris

The idea of an underground railway to relieve the congestion on the Paris streets was first proposed in 1855 but was only taken seriously after the siege of Paris by the Germans in 1871 during the Franco-Prussian War. A law passed in July 1865 granted local authorities all over France the power to build railways in their own local interest. In 1872 the City of Paris proposed to build an urban network of underground lines to improve public transport but permission was refused by the Minister of Public Works. Mindful of the strategic importance of a rail network in times of war, the government wanted the City Council to build the subway as an extension of the mainline network rather than as a separate system, but this would not best serve the interests of Paris. This difference of views prevailed for many years until 1895, when the Great Exhibition of 1900 was being organized and public transport became a priority. The government admitted defeat and allowed the city to build its Métro on condition that it would serve the exhibition sites as well as local interests.

On 9 July 1897 the city formally accepted the plan for a network of six lines covering a total length of 65km (41 miles), whose trains would be powered by electricity. Work began in 1898 on Line 1, which ran from Porte de Vincennes to Port Maillot on an east–west axis through the city. The tunnel was excavated using the Belgian or flying-arch method, in which a small section of the roof of the tunnel is excavated first, then propped as the arch is bricked over, before the excavation is widened and the next section of wall is built. This method was widely used before the tunnelling shield became popular because of its great economy. Unfortunately, despite the excellent progress made with tunnel excavation, Line 1 was not ready in time for the Great Exhibition in April 1900. But it did open in July of that year and in its first six months of operation carried almost four million people.

The River Seine occupies a central position through the City and inevitably the Métro has to cross it to serve the communities of the left and right banks. These crossings can be made above ground on viaducts or underground by tunnelling. In the early years of the Paris Métro it was felt that the tunnelling technology was insufficiently advanced to tunnel under the River Seine and for that reason the original six lines were built to cross the river on viaducts. In later years, as the network was extended, conventional tunnelling techniques were used to burrow under the Seine, the canals, and tributary rivers.

The carriages and rolling stock were built like tram cars, with wooden bodies that were 8m (26ft) long carrying 40 passengers, and rode on four-wheeled bogies, with the traction coach operated by two 125hp electric motors. The first trains on Line 1 comprised a traction coach and two trailer coaches, but this formation soon proved inadequate to cope with the passenger numbers and was modified. On line 2 seven- and eight-car trains were used to take the increased passenger flows. An order for 283 cars was placed in 1903 for the rest of the network. But on 10 August that year an event took place that would alter the way that all rolling stock construction was to develop.

Towards the end of the evening rush hour, a short circuit in the motor of the leading car standing at Boulevard Barbes Station on Line 2 caused a small fire to break out and the wooden parts of the chassis to smoulder. The station staff decided to use the following train to shunt the smoking train to a siding at Belleville after disembarking passengers from both. The two trains set off with clouds of black smoke issuing

out of the burning motor. Unfortunately the points were not set for the train to be shunted to the siding and so the convoy carried on to the terminus at Nation. The smouldering train was in a tunnel section at Menilmontant when a raging fire broke out. The train that had followed behind had stopped at the previous station to disembark passengers from the two empty trains ahead. Whether the station master had a premonition, or noticed smoke blowing back into the station from the tunnel entrance, he asked all passengers to leave the train. Most ignored his advice and in the next few moments black smoke billowed out of the tunnel, killing 84 people.

the rise of the metro

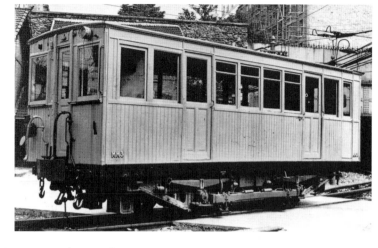

The wooden bodies of the cars and overheating, underpowered motors were felt to be the principal causes of the disaster and it was decided to convert all motorized wooden cars to trailer coaches. As a temporary measure, train lengths were reduced to seven coaches and the two motorized coaches were placed together at the head of the train, instead of one at the front and one at the back. In 1908, following extensive trials, the Paris Métro ordered the Sprague Thomson system: the driving compartment and switchgear of the wooden cars were encased in metal and the double-traction motors operated by a small master controller. This gave the train an easy and smooth acceleration and allowed the grouping of motors to work in tandem or as single units so that should one fail it did not incapacitate the train. This traction control gave the Paris Métro 75 years of reliable service, enabling it to withstand the overcrowding and minimal maintenance it received during the years of World War II.

Unlike those of most other subway systems, the trains of the Paris Métro run on rubber-tyred wheels and a wide flat steel rail. The system was gradually brought into service from 1959 after French engineers concluded that rubber-tyred trains could operate at faster speeds travelling between closely spaced stations, as they have higher acceleration and deceleration rates due to the greater friction between the rail and tyre. Conversion began with the short Line 11 and took 20 years to complete. It was a novel idea, enabling the existing line capacity to be increased without the need to lengthen station platforms or trains. Further savings were made by adapting existing rolling stock with the new wheel arrangement. The big expense was laying mile upon mile of new track and adding eight rubber wheels to each bogie.

Today there are 14 Metro lines, the latest of which is the Météor, the first phase of which opened in 1998, increasing the overall Métro and RER track length to 209km (130 miles). The Météor differs in many important respects from other lines on the network: the operation of the trains is entirely automatic; the platforms are isolated from the tracks by glass partition walls, which slide open when the trains stop; and the average distance between stations is now 2km (1¼ miles), as opposed to 500–700m (547–766yds) on other lines, allowing an average train speed of 40kph (25mph) against 25kph (16mph) on the older lines. The eight-car trains and higher operation speed means the Météor can transport up to 40,000 passengers per hour. Stations on the Météor also break with tradition: no longer simply cylindrical corridors and platform spaces with tiled surfaces, they are structures of architectural character and great charm.

left **The robust concrete walls and steel roof construction of the U–Bahn, engineered to avoid undermining adjacent building foundations.**

below **Wood and concrete piles were driven into firm ground to support the tunnels below street level.**

berlin

It was the entrepreneur Werner von Siemens – who had built the first electrically powered tramway in the world in Berlin in 1881 – who first put forward the idea of building an electrically powered rapid transit railway for Berlin. In his first presentation of the scheme to the Berlin Municipality he proposed to build an elevated system that would run on viaducts down both sides of the street pavement to avoid excavating below ground. This proposal, based on his tram line, met with considerable public opposition. Eventually a revised scheme, with a third of the route taken underground below the central city streets, won approval.

Work on the "U-Bahn" started in 1896 after a co-operative body was set up between the Seimens group and their joint-venture partners Halske and Deutsche Bank. The consortium financed and built the railway and were allowed to earn a good return by running the network privately for the first seven years of its operation. The first U-Bahn lines travelled from Warschauer Brüke in the east to Uhlandstrasse via the Zoological Gardens in the west, and branch lines were taken north to Potsdamer Platz and south to Innsbrucker Platz. The U-Bahn opened in stages in 1902 as each section of the line was built. But the network programme did not stop there – while construction of the first lines and the 13 stations were in full swing, plans were agreed and work started on further expansion of the network. By the end of 1910 the network had gone from 11.2km to 35km (7 to 22 miles) of track and the expansion only stopped at the onset of World War I.

The city of Berlin is built on the marshy basin of the River Spree, on a subsoil of sand and gravel that is capable of supporting massive buildings. But it has a high water table – 5m (16ft 6in) below ground level north of the river and 2m (6ft 6in) on the south side – which formed an obstacle to deep underground excavation. However, at the end of the 1870s deep wells were dug for the extraction of drinking water and it was noticed subsequently that the ground water level had dropped. This showed that such deep wells could be employed to temporarily lower the ground water level local to a deep excavation. The engineers of the U-Bahn pioneered the science of ground water lowering to enable the trenches of the cut and cover tunnels to be excavated in the dry.

There were, however, other engineering problems to overcome. The wooden bulkheads

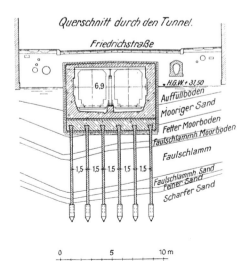

that were to enclose the tunnel trenches were not easy to drive into the tightly packed sand and gravel soil on Tauentzienstrasse and caused vibrations to the neighbouring houses and cracks to form in the roadway. Further difficulties occurred on Kleiststrasse, where the marl lying near the surface was covered with stone cobbles, which imposed limits on the piles that were needed to support the foundation plate. The U-Bahn line came close to the Kaiser Wilhelm memorial church and to protect it double T-shaped iron girders were driven into the ground at intervals and the gaps between them lined with horizontal timber boards. The resulting trench side walls were braced against each other by round timber poles acting as struts.

Although the state of the ground changed frequently, this method of tunnel construction was simple and reliable to use. Where the road could be closed to traffic, the excavation was left open in the interests of carrying on further construction work, otherwise it had to be covered over with a temporary roof, so that traffic could continue to circulate freely.

The early U-Bahn tunnels had an outer watertight sheath around their entire perimeter. Its thickness depended on how deep it was below the ground water table and on the earth pressures acting against the tunnel body. It had to be watertight even under pressure or corrosive or acidic ground conditions and sufficiently flexible to enable it to reliably overcome the small movements and fine cracks that inevitably occur in tunnel walls. The protective sheath was composed of several layers of asphalt and bitumen-impregnated paper, which were joined

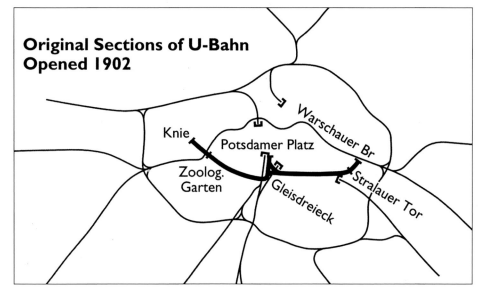

Original Sections of U-Bahn Opened 1902

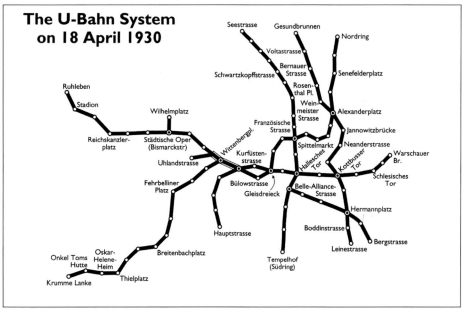

The U-Bahn System on 18 April 1930

together using a hot viscous adhesive on site. The tunnel walls and the floor slab were constructed of reinforced concrete, the tunnel roof formed from double T-shaped iron girders spanning from wall to wall and capped by a concrete layer between them.

Where there was ground settlement, or the excavation could undermine adjacent buildings, a foundation plate was laid underneath the tunnel slab floor, which rested on wooden stakes (or reinforced concrete ones in areas of high acidity), which were pile driven into firmer ground below.

From 1920 onwards all new routes of the underground carried wider and longer cars to increase passenger capacity. Although these new cars ran on the same track width as the older ones, the two were not interchangeable. Extension to the small-profile train network continued until 1929, when the system had achieved it full potential. The Berlin U-Bahn still operates two types of rolling stock on its nine

lines: the small-profile (*Kleinprofil*) trains run on the original lines, now called U1, U2, U4, and U15 lines, while the larger stock (*Grossprofil*) is found on lines U5–U9. The larger cars are 2.65m (8ft 8in) wide, 16m (52ft 6in) long, and can travel at speeds of up to 60kph (37mph), while the small-profile ones are 2.35m (7ft 9in) wide, 12.6m (41ft 4in) long, and have a maximum speed of 50kph (31mph). A further distinction is that the large-profile trains can take current from either an overhead cable or from the third rail.

The line of the small-profile train generally served the east–west axis of the city, while the north–south traffic was handled by the tramways, which were congesting the streets. The large-profile trains were built to create a network of two new lines that crossed the city on a north-south axis. The work progressed in fits and starts due to the onset of World War I and the raging inflation that hit the German economy thereafter. The first 4km (2½ miles) of

the rise of the metro

left **An architectural sketch of a New York street viaduct modelled on the Charlottenburg extension of the U-Bahn.**

below **A class B1 large-profile train, c.1924. With their two oval end windows these trains gained the nickname** *Tunneleulen* **(tunnel owls).**

track opened in 1923 and the last extension to the network to Tempelhof was completed in1930. With the opening of the borders between East and West Berlin quite a lot of reconstruction and reconfiguration work took place from 1989 to facilitate travel across the newly unified city.

The early small-profile car had a chassis made of wood, which was mounted onto a steel underframe. Wooden seats were provided for third-class passengers, upholstered seats in second-class and in the smoking lounges for first-class clients. A three-car train could carry a total of 210 passengers, of whom 122 could be seated. The early train formation of a trailer car between two motor cars was found to be inadequate to pull the trains efficiently, and so subsequently trains had four motors to drive each motor car and ran in a four-car formation with a motor car at either end of the train.

The U-Bahn is operated by direct current supplied to the third rail at 750 volts. The electricity is supplied by a local power supply company, BEWAG, and transformed down to the many substations of the U-Bahn. The BVG (Berliner Verkehrsbetriebe), who control the U-Bahn network today, have a central control room that monitors and balances the power from the substations, which are located every 2–4km (1½–2½ miles) along the various lines. Normally a substation will provide two sections of the line with current, but where two lines cross it may supply up to four.

All trains currently serving the U-Bahn are built of aluminium and run with six cars that are inter-connected by a central corridor, which allows an unimpeded view the length of the train. The interior finishes, seat covers, and panelling are made from fire- and tear-resistant material that can be recycled. One of the features of the latest stock of large-profile trains is that the driver cab has the largest area of toughened clear glazing (79 per cent) of any metro in the world.

new york

While New York spent years debating, pondering, and politicizing over the commissioning of a subway system, the cities of Boston, Glasgow, Budapest, and Paris had started building their underground railways. The most important city of the USA was falling behind in modernizing and improving its congested transport infrastructure. Finally, in 1898, a scheme proposed by William Barclay Parsons – one of the foremost civil engineers of his day –

was approved, and he was appointed as Chief Engineer.

The geology of Manhattan revealed that hard rock outcropped at about 4.5–6m (15–20ft) below ground, and in some places it was very near the surface. Parsons had recommended electrifying the line rather than using coal-burning locomotives – besides being cleaner he felt it would be cheaper to operate. Tunnelling through rock was going to be expensive and

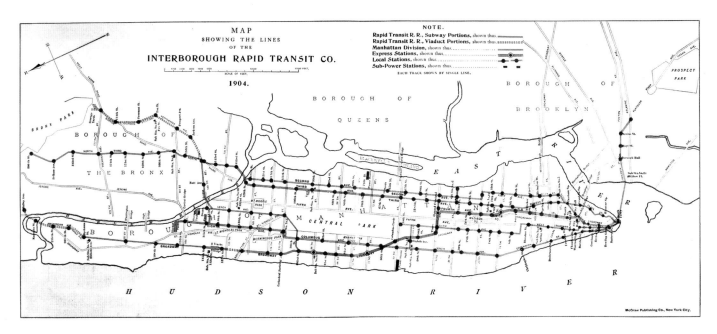

the rise of the metro

slow, so Parsons took the bold decision to keep the subway at a shallow depth below street level. This meant that in areas where the topography of the surface sloped away quite abruptly, the railway would have to run above ground level on viaduct running down the main street.

Building technology was so primitive a hundred years ago that the excavation had to carried out entirely by hand – 7,000 labourers made up the workforce at its peak. The men led a hard life, earning $2–$2.50 a day, and there were many accidents, tunnel collapses, and fatalities. Probably the unluckiest individual was Major Ira Shaler, who was a tunnelling subcontractor for a section of the subway. His first calamity occurred when a building

containing 90kg (200lb) of dynamite caught fire and exploded. The blast wrecked the Murray Hotel, damaged Grand Central Station, and shattered glass on a number of nearby buildings, killing five people and injuring more than 100. Two months later a tunnel collapsed during the early hours of the morning. It partially filled the tunnel with rubble and boulders, delaying the project by several weeks and undermining the foundation of four luxury houses on Murray Hill, for which Shaler had to pay compensation. Three months later Shaler was struck by a large boulder, which broke his neck. He died in hospital 11 days later.

On 27 October 1904 Mayor George McClellan switched on the motor, turned the

below **The shallow depth of excavation meant that many buildings had to be shored up and water mains and drains temporarily diverted.**

bottom **An early New York steel passenger car. It was 15½ metres (51 ft) long and could seat 52 passengers.**

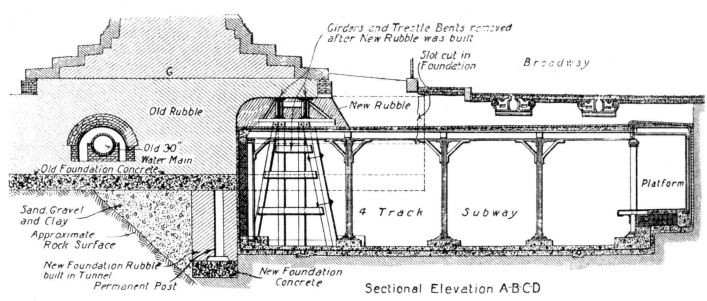

Sectional Elevation A·B·C·D

controller in the driver's cab, and headed the first train of the New York subway north for a tour of the Interborough Rapid Transit. An English expert who was there remarked that it was "one of the great engineering achievements of the age" and acknowledged that it was more advanced technologically than the London underground, although not as large. The IRT was certainly the longest subway system completed at a single time, covering 35 km (22 miles).

Before the subway was built, New York had quite an extensive network of elevated metro Lines driven by steam engines, serving Manhattan Island and the outlying boroughs of Brooklyn and Queens. The elevated trains were run by two private companies: the Manhattan Railway Company and the Brooklyn Rapid Transit (BRT). The trains dominated the

streetscape and, as the lines expanded and grew, obstructed the smooth flow of road traffic through the city centre. So from 1900, it was decided to build the metro system underground and gradually replace and dismantle the elevated street system, all of which had disappeared by the end of 1932. The City of New York slowly began to take control of the subway and bus operations and by 1953 the public transport system of New York and the surrounding boroughs was run by just one body: the New York City Transit Authority. The NYCTA was responsible for a subway network as extensive as London's, serving 486 stations and covering 384km (240 miles) of track. In 1968 the NYCTA in turn came under the jurisdiction of the Metropolitan Transportation Authority, which also controlled the Staten Island Rapid Transit

right **The electricity to run
the system was generated
by special coal-burning
power stations.**

below **The steel-framed
chassis of an early
passenger car.**

and Long Island Railroad, which connected
Manhattan to the State of Jersey. Today there are
three lines serving the City of New York and
Manhattan: the Brooklyn Manhattan Transit line
(BMT), the Independent Line (IND), and the old
Interborough Rapid Transit line.

In the 1970s the NYCTA cars were
characterized by their shiny stainless-steel
coachwork and their moulded glass-fibre
interior seating. Every year more network and
stations were added, the trains stretched and
grew longer, and more passengers were carried
on the same track and in the same ageing
rolling stock until the system slowly but surely
began to deteriorate from overload and
breakdown. In 1981 the New York State
Legislature finally declared a transport
emergency and injected massive funds into
rehabilitating its 56 stations and modernizing
the run-down and outmoded infrastructure of
the subway system. New cars and equipment
were bought from Japan, Canada, and France,
many miles of new track were laid, and new
tunnels were excavated to create the extra
capacity the subway required to meet projected
future passenger traffic levels.

This undertaking was undoubtedly prompted
by the public humiliation that the USA and
NYCTA had suffered in the press address given by
Deputy Prime Minister Kozlov of the USSR
during the American National Exhibition in
Moscow in the summer of 1959. Kozlov had
described the IRT, BMT, and IND lines as "lousy",
and complained that "the subways are dirty and
the air bad – very bad." Asked how New York's
underground could be improved, Kozlov said it
was beyond repair: "You would just have to
reconstruct it, I think."

The reconstruction work that began in the
'70s was endangered by the weak economy in
the USA in the '90s and increased competition
from private cars and cheap bus services. But
despite the competition, the subway is still the
most popular way for office workers to commute
to the city every day. The subway caters for some
2.7 million passengers daily, and with 1,155km
(722 miles) of track, New York has probably the
longest metro network in the world.

Two features that distinguish the New York
subway from most other rapid-transit systems
around the world – multi-tracking and two-
directional signalling – have helped to reduce
serious breakdowns of the system.

below, left **Boys play on the roof of a tunnel section submerged in the temporary canal in Hofplein Square.**

below, right **The more economical rectangular sections (top) were used under the streets, where they did not need to withstand water pressure.**

bottom **Sections of tunnel being built in a specially constructed dry dock on the site of a department store that was bombed in World War II.**

rotterdam

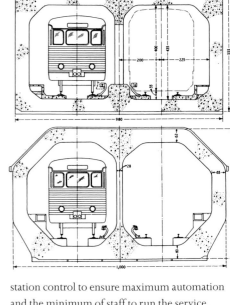

Although Rotterdam was the first city in the Netherlands to have a metro, it lagged behind the other major European centres in introducing underground travel. This was due largely to the land being flat and low lying, the city split by the River Maas waterways, and the high cost of conventional deep tunnel excavation. Rotterdam's public transport was initially served by horse-drawn trams in the early 1900s, to be replaced by electric trams by the 1920s and supplemented by motorized buses ten years later. Traffic congestion clogged the streets for many years as the city expanded and grew as Europe's largest sea-going port. World War II decimated the city and the bridges that spanned the river. There were many bridges to rebuild after the War, but even when they were re-opened and existing road tunnel was back in use, there were long delays during the rush hour or when a bridge closed every two hours for shipping. Such problems made Rotterdam City Council look at alternative forms of public transport and visits were made to New York, Toronto, and Cleveland to study modern signalling methods and the use of CCTV for station control to ensure maximum automation and the minimum of staff to run the service.

Dutch engineers devised a unique tunnelling method – Immersed Tube Construction – to make river and canal crossings by laying completed tunnel segments along the bed of the river. The region's subsoil conditions of peat and clay overlying sand make this construction method very economic as it minimizes excavation. When the Rotterdam metro was being built under the River Maas, a huge dry dock was constructed for precasting the twin tunnel segments. They were cast in small units then joined together to form 90m (300ft) long sections that weighed 4,500 tons. The concrete units were linked together by rubber gaskets that were squeezed tight by prestressing from either end to make them watertight, after temporary steel bulk heads were formed at the open ends.

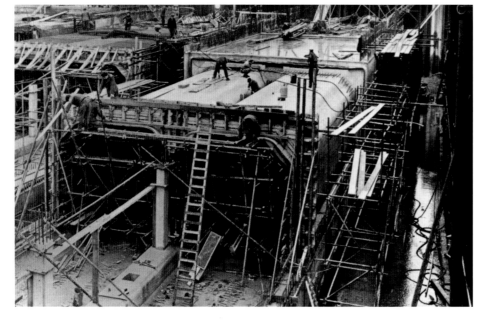

The dry dock was flooded after carefully ballasting the segments to ensure they floated only a few inches above the water line. They were then towed to the exact position and sunk onto pile heads installed on the hollowed out river bed before anchoring them down. Finally the sections were winched together under pressure, water was pumped out from between the bulk heads, and the track was laid. The central portion of the tunnel on the river bed was 200m (650ft) long, rising on a slight gradient toward Rijnhaven to the south with the track some 18m (60ft) below the water line. To the north the tunnel remained underground until it reached the terminus at Central Station. South of the river the metro continued on elevated viaducts to Zuidplein, traversing a distance of 5.9km (3½ miles). To form the tunnel section along the centre of a wide avenue called the Coolsingal a special canal was excavated down the middle of the road, then flooded to allow the prefabricated tunnel sections to be floated into position, submerged, connected, then pumped dry.

After nine years, building work was finally completed. The first line with its seven stations between Central Station and Zuidplein was officially opened on 9 February 1968 by Princess Beatrix. To mark the opening, every household in Rotterdam was sent a letter from The Mayor, enclosing a free ticket.

Over the past 30 years, as the city of Rotterdam has developed and expanded further, the Rotterdam Transport Authority, RET, has kept pace with this growth, providing the transport network for not only Rotterdam, but also other neighbouring municipalities. RET now operates ten tram lines, 33 bus services, and 11 night services, plus 79.2km (49 miles) of metro routes. The first metro line built is now called the Erasmus Line and runs north– south across the city and then westward to De Akkers south of the river. An east–west route north of the river, called the Caland Line, was added later, running from Marconiplein in the west to De Terp, with spur lines running northward to De Tachen and Binnehof. In the current transport plan the metro has been extended further westward by the new Benelux Line and eastward by the Nesseland Line, with a high speed light rail being built to link Rotterdam with the Hague and Zoetemeer to provide a fast commuter service to the suburbs.

RET has introduced CCTV in trams and buses to monitor social problems. Also, in response to the number of serious metro tunnel accidents that have occurred in Europe over the past decade, and particularly the fire in a tunnel at Haverstraat in 1998, fire safety procedures were drawn up by RET and displayed in all metro trains and stations.

above **A modern train pulls into Wilhelminaplein, a station opened in 1997 to serve new city developments in Rotterdam's docklands.**

below **The building dock on Brienenoord Island with one of the tunnel sections being towed out, 1965.**

station
art and
architecture

berlin

station art and architecture

The architect Alfred Grenander was responsible for most of the original station and viaduct designs of the U-Bahn in Berlin. He was appointed by the first director of the U-Bahn, Paul Wittig, who himself was an architect and had been project architect in the building of the Reichstag in 1894. In general, the high-level structures were designed with rich detailing and ornamentation in the decorative style of the Wilhelmine Period, sometimes referred to as the German Renaissance. Grenander later revised his design ideas to embrace the purity and functionalism of the Bauhaus or Modern Movement, inspired by Walter Gropius. From 1919 onward the buildings of the U-Bahn were stark and unadorned, the architecture exploiting the material properties of brick and concrete to derive an aesthetic. There may have been a more telling reason for this change, however, namely the material shortages and financial constraints imposed in the aftermath of World War I.

The most striking feature of the Berlin U-Bahn was the architectural development of the high-level railway. The basic question that troubled the designers was whether it was socially acceptable to build an "underground" railway where most of it would be visible above ground and at high-level, running down and across the streets of Berlin. Underground enthusiasts insisted that the city and its streets would be blighted by an ugly high-level railway with its gaunt iron structure. The economic arguments for a high-level metro and the existence of well-designed and pleasing iron viaducts in other cities gradually won the sceptics over. They came around to the idea that these great works could have much to offer in terms of artistic merit. They would avoid the utilitarian designs of the high-level railway schemes of New York, Liverpool, and Chicago, where the functional needs of the construction were stamped on their external appearance.

So the high-level sections of the U-Bahn became architecturally modelled and well defined in terms of aesthetic and visual impact. Although the viaducts straddling the pavements were first conceived as a mass of supporting piers without decoration or ornamentation, gradually more and more stonework was added, while the moulding of the girders was constantly being improved. For example, from Potsdamer Strasse to Nollendorfplatz the supporting legs of the viaduct were deliberately splayed outward, giving the impression that the pathway running beneath for vehicles and pedestrians was wide and open. The proportioning and shaping of these viaducts and the trussed spans emphasize the fluidity, strength, and ductility of their metal fabrication. The bridge over the Landwehr Canal, with its 70m- (230ft-) wide span, is a charming example of what can be achieved artistically from an intrinsically prosaic girder trellis. By strongly emphasizing the end supports, a more pronounced connection with the cross-beams supporting the bridge was created.

The design for Hallesches Tor station presented particular difficulties, because the comparatively narrow width of the street at that point required that the station be shifted as far as possible toward the bank of the Landwehr Canal. Nevertheless, the piers on the waterside still stand out from the sweep of the canal and the station hall itself towers magnificently over the

right **The new realism of the Modern Movement was manifest in the severe brick-faced entrance structure to Olympia-Stadion's entrance hall, built in 1930.**

above **This rendering of the all-brick entrance hall to Gesundbrunnen station, with its flat roof and horizontal strip windows, shows the transformation in architectural style that occurred in the late 1920s, embracing the Modern Movement.**

surface of the water. The problem of producing a monumental effect in this narrow space was further addressed by giving the station hall a rich sandstone appearance on the east side, which is reflected in the piers of the Hallesches Tor Bridge on the other side, thus bringing the two elements into a unified whole.

Nollendorfplatz station, at the western end of the high-level railway system, is topped with a dome that dominates the area from the middle of the square below it. From this dome structure the railway travels underground, first across an iron viaduct, then a stone ramp, before it dives under the viaduct. The open cut of the ramp is enclosed

by a wonderful balustrade flanked by two sandstone columns at the tunnel entrance.

In general, the tight spaces prescribed for the below-ground stations left little scope or need for decoration and embellishment. Everything was out of sight except for the station's entrance, which would probably be covered in brickwork or washable hardwearing tiles, as would the platform walls. In the later years, from 1919 to 1930, when the original small profile network of the U-Bahn was completed, the appearance of underground station entrances transformed from a highly decorative style to one of stark functionalism to embrace the Modern Movement.

left **The interior opulence of the vaulted canopy ceiling and column supports to the platforms at Heidelberger Platz may have inspired the architects of the Moscow metro.**

right **Krumme Lanke station entrance, built in 1929, was a real breakthrough in style, the concrete structure becoming the focus of its external expression. This station undoubtedly influenced many London Underground stations built in the 1930s.**

right **The arched ceiling
over the main concourse of
Elektrozavodska station
epitomizes the timeless
beauty and handcrafted
quality of the surface
detailing on the Moscow
metro stations.**

below **The drawing shows
the richly decorated stone
façades to the entrance to
Sokolniki station, which
marked a return to the Art
Nouveau and Expressionist
styles of a decade earlier.**

moscow

"Our Metropolitan Railway is a prototype of the general socialist organization of public services, and this is its great historical significance. The construction of the metro inaugurates a new and higher phase of Soviet architecture, which will be manifested in the reconstruction of Moscow." So read the Moscow City Council statement about the new underground railway intended to glorify socialism and the Stalinist regime.

Without question this is one of the finest collections of underground stations ever built. In scale, grandeur, and spaciousness the architecture of the Moscow metro was way ahead of anything ever built up to that period. Seventy years on, its beauty can still make many modern metro stations look drab and unexciting. The following informative and wonderfully atmospheric passages are translated from the commemorative book published in 1936:

In order to make Moscow a city worthy of the title Capital of the Socialist Motherhood and Centre of the Worldwide Proletarian Revolution, and to turn Moscow from a large shabby village into a socialist city, Moscow Bolsheviks had to solve a mammoth building task in the shortest possible time. By way of example we looked at the metros of London and New York and concluded that with the exception of some recent London underground stations, they were all generally dirty, run down, and dull to look at. It seems that in capitalist countries it is considered pointless to spend more than the bare minimum on a public service. In the Soviet Union we have a completely different attitude: we want to make a passenger's journey on the underground not only as comfortable but also as enjoyable as possible.

We have striven to individualize the outward appearance of our stations so that passengers find it easier to see where they are from inside the carriages. Polished marble and granite of different hues were the materials we chose to cover the walls, the ceiling, and columns of the stations. The Moscow metro was built with local materials, local labour, and Soviet-made trains and equipment.

Apart from the artistic requirements in making the Moscow metro the most beautiful in the world, there were special operational requirements such as the need to have walls which are resistant against damp, which are easy to clean, would not allow dust to gather, and are durable and hard wearing. This made it necessary to use high-quality materials such as polished marble and granite.

The design of the metro stations was determined by a single and overriding

below **The colonnade at Komsomolskaya station at platform level, with its polished marble surfaces and delicate glass ceiling lights, could easily be mistaken for the interior of an opulent stately home.**

below, top **An original sketch drawing of the interior view of the ticket hall at Sokolniki station.**

below, bottom **A view of the platform concourse of Okhotny Ryad station with elegant floor-mounted uplighters. The design of this station was probably copied and remodelled by London Underground for Gants Hill station.**

above **A long, beautifully illuminated escalator at Komsomolskaya on the Circle Line, perhaps the most opulent of all Moscow's stations.**

creative notion which was accepted unconditionally by all the architects without exception. The underground structures should not look like underground structures, they should not remind people of being below the surface without daylight. The stations should be filled with light, should feel spacious, and should be bright and happy places.

Neo-classical architecture was used in a self-conscious way to dress the internal walls and ceilings of the stations. The Modern Movement and all that it symbolized was rejected, and along with it the influence of some fine Russian architects such as Tatlin and Melnokov. During the Lenin era they had both pioneered avant-garde freestyle architecture that broke way from

traditional and historical references. The Moscow metro was designed at the beginning of the Stalin oligarchy and was a retrogressive return to an architecture with a recognizable identity and that was full of imperialist ambition. One feels privileged and humbled as an individual walking into these palatial surroundings today, but one wonders how such lavish decoration was perceived by the low-waged State workers living under such an oppressive regime.

Construction work started in 1932 with the east–west line between Sokolniki and Gorky Park opening in 1935. The present network of three through routes and a circle line linking them together was completed in the 1960s. Today, the Moscow metro has the fourth largest network in the world and carries more passengers per year than any other.

far left **One of the familiar "ballroom" interiors of the Moscow metro – this one belongs to Komsomolskaya station and includes a finely plastered ceiling, enamelled inlay panels, and white stone-clad octagonal supporting columns. The focal point is the series of brass chandeliers, which illuminate the station.**

left, top and bottom **In Mayakovskaya station the architecture moves away from excessive adornment to bring greater cohesion to the internal space. The curvature of the arches springing from columns in both directions is emphasized by a ribbon of darker tiles. The unity, openness, and subtle proportion of this elegant concourse is helped by recessing the large circular light wells into the roof. Below is a detail of a stained-glass window.**

piccadilly line extension, london

The 1930s saw the emergence of a new architecture in Europe – Modernism, or Functionalism, as it was sometimes called – that triggered a significant change in the design of London's underground stations. It was during this period that architect Charles Holden and Frank Pick, the chief executive of London Transport, made an architectural tour of European cities before finalizing the master plan for a major extension of the Piccadilly Line to the northern suburbs of London. They visited Amsterdam to study the De Stijl movement, Weimar and Berlin to find out about the Bauhaus, and Sweden and Denmark for further architectural inspiration.

Throughout Western Europe at that time, railway companies were adopting the German plan of placing stations in a spacious setting so that they became the focal point of a town and a transport hub for trains, buses, and cars. This was a significant advance in the field of suburban station planning that British architects had largely ignored, preferring to design suburban stations that slotted in with the existing streetscape, that looked like shop fronts, houses, or doorways leading into a department store or other building.

Functionalism rejected unnecessary decoration of a building, believing that good

architecture derived solely from the proportion, scale, and arrangement of building form. The rapid advances in construction technology and the introduction of new building materials – steel, reinforced concrete, and glass – together with lightweight tensile frame construction, began liberating architecture from the many restrictions imposed by load-bearing brickwork and masonry construction. The superior strength of concrete and steel made it possible to widen the floor span, to enlarge window openings, and to increase the lightness and transparency of a structure.

Holden saw a great many Modern buildings on the tour and on his return to London set about defining the qualities that would best suit the architecture of a modern underground station. He did not want to copy the work of

other architects but was committed to finding an architecture that was simple, honest, and pure in form. He wanted to design well-proportioned structures of uncomplicated yet harmonious shape, believing that "the use of clear simple forms imparts to the stations an air of authority and makes them easily recognizable".

Holden chose to use brickwork for both the interior and the exterior cladding of the new concrete-framed stations, feeling that it would project warmth and would be appreciated for its traditional qualities. It would also be a great deal cheaper than stone. Large plate-glass clerestory windows mounted in steel frames were inserted over the entrances to introduce good natural daylight into the buildings. Uplighters were used to bathe the ceiling and walls in warm light

above **The new suburban architecture pioneered by Holden for Sudbury Town station was influenced by the Modern Movement and shows Holden's preference for brick–faced structures built in concrete and featuring large clerestory windows. By night the internal lighting floodlights the street as well as the station interior.**

below, left **The illuminated rotunda of Southgate's ticket hall.**

below, right **The symmetry and grace of Arnos Grove station has been compared to the Stockholm Public Library, designed by Erik Asplund in 1928, which Holden greatly admired.**

above **The escalators leading down to the platforms at Southgate station. Their bronze pedestal uplighters were retained when the escalators were modernized in the 1980s.**

without glare, and by night illuminated the large windows like beacons.

The tiling used for the interior walls varied between locations but was predominantly a warm cream glaze – like that used on the Berlin U-Bahn – which enhanced the glow from the uplighting. White pressed-cement tiles were used for the floor covering, along with terrazzo. Bronze and similar durable metal alloys replaced wood for the hand railings, stair treads, poster frames, and turnstiles. Signs and notices were to have a corporate colour scheme and be integrated into the overall station design. The location and grouping of advertising and

publicity posters was to be given careful consideration, because this would increase the revenue from stations. Also, it was felt that if properly positioned, posters could add an attractive mural effect. Provision for vending machines, telephone booths, and newspaper kiosks was designed as part of the architecture, rather than added on as an afterthought.

With stations like Arnos Grove, Sudbury Town, and Southgate, Charles Holden brought the Piccadilly Line Extension of the 1930s into the forefront of Modern station architecture – an architecture that has never been bettered by an English railway company.

right **At Rinkeby, the artist Nils Zetterberg transformed the station into a cave full of prehistoric finds. Tiny objects have been blown up to large mosaics glittering with gold; there are runic inscriptions and paintings of flying birds.**

far right **Stadion station was the last of the cave interiors to be built, in 1975. The entrance archway was painted as a rainbow of hope by artists Enno Hallek and Ake Pallarp.**

right, bottom **P. Ultvedt's bright blue leaf motif, which is painted on the cavelike structure of the platforms and concourse of the Blue Line at T–Centralen station.**

stockholm

The longest art gallery in the world, the greatest art show on the planet, where subway architecture becomes art – these are all ways in which art lovers the world over have described the Stockholm metro stations. How did such a dream of an idea become a reality? Who convinced a body of sober government officials – inevitably averse to radical change or unnecessary expenditure – to give a group of artists the freedom to express their fantasies on the walls, ceilings, and platforms of 90 costly underground stations?

Swedish artists Siri Derkert and Vera Nilsson delivered many articulate and persuasive arguments to the railway board and local council during the time the metro was being planned. This resulted in two motions being submitted to the Stockholm City Council in 1955 for debate. One of them read:

Although it may not be possible to turn each underground station into a fairytale castle, artists, sculptors, potters, and craftsmen should, in association with architects and engineers, nevertheless be given the opportunity to create beautiful rooms and stimulating station environments throughout, and also mould one of the main stations into an underground cathedral with a fanfare of colour and rhythm.

All political parties rallied in favour of the motion, and shortly afterward, in March 1956, a competition to decorate T-Centralen, the main station, was announced. In the years that followed, a series of art works were implemented on the upper platforms and in the ticket halls of the station. The whole enterprise was a great success: art as an architectural concept became rooted in the Stockholm metro and continued to flourish in the rest of the stations as they were built, though T-Centralen still contains more works of art and sculpture than any other station on the network.

The deep underground stations of the Stockholm metro were excavated through dense self-supporting bedrock, and the cavernous spaces that were created became the inspiration for a group of Swedish artists calling themselves "the concretists". As the name implies, their art was sculpted, sandblasted, and painted onto the sprayed concrete lining that protected the rough, tooled face of the tunnels. For the Blue Line platform in T-Centralen station, the roof and walls combine to form a single arch excavated out of the bedrock onto which a 7cm (3in) layer

left **The "Sky of Cubes" is the title of artist Takashi Naraha's design for Vreten station, which was built in 1985. The cubes depict patches of summer sky and are positioned on the roof and walls of this deep underground station.**

above **Artist Gun Gordillo used white neon lighting strips to illuminate the ceiling of the central platform at Hötorget station.**

right, top **At Ostermalmstorg station, which opened in 1965, light-coloured concrete was sandblasted by Siri Derkert to create pictures of dancing, playing, and singing figures and caricatures of some well-known women from the past.**

right, bottom **At Skarpnack, one of the later stations to be opened, sculptor Richard Nonas designed a row of geometric stone seating plinths that run down the centre of the main platform. From here the seated passenger has a view of the entire length of the station.**

of concrete was sprayed. The surface was then painted by Per Ultvedt in blue and white, criss-crossed with a leaf motif reminiscent of the old murals found in provincial churches. Meanwhile, at Ostermalmstorg station in 1961 artist Siri Derkert's competition-winning design titled "Gougings in Natural Concrete" was a series of Picasso-like sketches and doodles sandblasted by the artist onto the hardened concrete walls. At the age of 73 she descended 36m (118ft) down into the cold tunnels to start sketching and sandblasting her series of cartoons along a 300m (984ft) stretch of wall.

The Stockholm metro that first opened in 1950 was an upgraded tram route. The first purpose-built metro line did not open until 1957, and over the years was extended to reach far into the city's suburbs. In 1965 a new underground network was designed to interconnect with buses and local trains to form a comprehensive public transport system for Greater Stockholm. Today there are three lines in operation – the Red, Blue, and Green lines. With a total route length of 110km (68 miles), and sculpture, mosaics, and paintings in 90 of the 100 stations along the network, the Stockholm metro truly can be regarded as the longest art exhibition in the world. The stations abound with arrays of stunning, outlandish, even overwhelming art work, ranging from a lush garden, a babbling spring, a suspended glass dodecagon, and a bronze cheetah to lighting designs, wall sculptures, ceramic decorations, murals, and fantasy rock structures. Next to such displays, the trains, platforms, and people can seem almost a mere sideshow.

right **A larger than lifesize portrait of the writer August Strindberg greets passengers as they exit Radmansgatan. The station is close to Strindberg's last home known as the Blue Tower, which is now a museum. This is the theme that artist Sture Valentin Nilsson chose for the station.**

station art and architecture

stockholm

washington

The Washington Metropolitan Area Transit Authority, better known as WMATA, operates the second largest rail transit system in the USA. It serves a population of 3.5 million people living within an area consisting of the District of Columbia, the suburban counties of Maryland and North Virginia, and the national capital itself. The authority was set up in 1967 to plan, build, finance, and operate a metro network of 174km (108 miles) consisting of five separate lines, 83 stations, and 843 railcars – all starting from scratch. The cost was a staggering 9.3 billion dollars, with the first phase opening in 1976 and the final leg of the network completed in 2001.

The most compelling feature of the metro is the coffered ceilings of all the subway stations. Five materials were selected – granite, red quarry tiles, concrete, glass, and bronze – to create a hierarchy of material usage and to develop a common identity within the architecture of the metro system. The long straight lengths of

platforms on either side of the tracks have flashing edge lights, which turn on as a train enters the station. Although functional – to improve safety – the effect is highly theatrical.

Despite the many constructional difficulties and the huge cost overruns, the Washington metro achieved an architecture that sets it apart from other systems in terms of continuity of design, standardization of construction detail, and symmetry of architecture. The maintenance costs are thus reduced because replacement parts like handrails, floor tiles, walls tiles, and light fittings are standard throughout the network.

The Chicago-based architect Harry Weese who was contracted to design the Washington stations introduced a coherent architecture to the internal spaces. Weese wanted every part of the metro system to be regarded as belonging to the womb of a 100-mile long piece of architecture. He conceived the idea of a single massive roof made up of waffled arches for all the underground

station art and architecture

stations, with all the lighting in the station directed upward onto the ceiling. The station roof was built as a plain reinforced concrete arch and finished with precast coffered panels to ensure a watertight construction.

Benjamin Fogey of the *Washington Post* summed up Weese's achievement in a tribute in 1998:

Washingtonians who use the subway regularly take for granted its clarity and beauty. Visitors always go ohh and ahh. . Sometimes even veteran users are taken aback. You are gliding up from the shadowy depths of the escalators at say the north exit from Judiciary Square station thinking about not very much. Suddenly the blue sky appears and the massive brick pediment of the Old Pension Building cuts into the blue, and then the whole amazing edifice fills your line of sight. Moments like this are enough to make a day, and the best part is that memories do not vanish in a blink. They enter your storehouse of spirit lifting moments. These are the aesthetic qualities that Harry Weese gave to the mundane experience of getting from here to there and makes the Washington metro so unforgettable.

below **The shapes and intense colours of Roger Somville's fresco "Notre Temps" at Hanker station can be unsettling. The influence of grafitti art seems clear.**

bottom, left **Paul De Gobert's work in Vandervelde station depicts rolling hills and broad plains to show how urban growth pushes back the natural world.**

bottom, right **This abstract sculpture – the work of Reinhoud d'Haese in Osseghem station – can be read many ways. One interpretation suggests a dynamic group of passengers locked in a scrum trying to force their way through with no one willing to let them pass.**

brussels

Like many other metros in Europe, Brussels started up as an underground tramway. There were initially two lines – Line 1 opened in 1969 and Line 2 in 1970 – which were converted to a full metro line after 1976. Today, Lines 1, 1A, 1B, and 2 are operated as full metro lines whereas the north–south city tunnel (Line 3) and outer ring tunnel in the east (Line 5) are still used by trams with low-station platforms. The 41km (25½ miles) of the metro network, which has more than 50 stations, is operated by STIB (Société de Transports Intercommunaux de Bruxelles), which is also responsible for a tram network of 133km (82½ miles), 12km (7½ miles) of which are in tunnels.

The Brussels metro has a well-earned reputation for encouraging works of contemporary art in its stations. Such is the importance of art in the metro that in 1990 the Minister for Public Works set up an independent arts commission that is responsible for recommending and approving art to all the transit facilities and sites in the Greater Brussels area. The commission acts as a censorship body to ensure that art on public display is sensitive to broad community values and good taste.

There certainly appears to have been greater freedom of expression for the artists' personalities and emotions in the art works created before the new arts committee was set up. In 1976, for example, Roger Somville painted a giant fresco on the walls and ceilings of Hanker station that overwhelms the onlooker. The work, which is titled "Notre Temps" (Our Time), evokes the struggle for a socially and economically fairer society. The shapes and intense colours of the fresco and the larger-than-life people depicted in the images are provocative and disturbing. Much the same could be said of the mesmerizing wall relief created at Botanique station by Emile Souply in 1979 in bold stripes of different colours to evoke old tram lines. Bands of coloured tubing in red, green, white, and yellow snake across the

wall faces, curving and coiling their way around corners. The motion of travel is auto-suggested by the interplay of primary colours on the retina.

Reinhold d'Haese's polymorphic sculpture "Stop The Run" at Ossenghem is a collage of organic forms evolved from giant plants crossed with animal heads and humanoid shapes – things one might imagine in a surrealist nightmare. The dormant masks of giant tulip heads seem to grow out of the walls of the station with a strange menacing presence. On a more lighthearted note, the lifesized cardboard caricature sculptures of commuters with staring eyes that are clustered in the entrance hall of Botanique station are the brainchild of artist Pierre Caille.

Art of more recent times includes the work of Phillip Decelle at Roi Baudouin station, which shows 31 stylized ducks flying over the platform ceiling, while at Tomberg station artists Guy Rombouts and Monica Droste have created abstract lettering on a wall of beautiful blue tiles, which is more restrained and less startling.

Thirty years after the first underground line was put into service, the Brussels metro has become a living museum. More than 60 works of art decorate its platforms and concourses. Every genre is represented – painting, sculpture, photography, stained glass – as well as a wealth of different materials, from canvas to bronze, and from wood to glass and steel. There is something for all artistic tastes on the Brussels metro. Surely this is how contemporary art can really connect with society and also brighten up a mundane trudge to and from work every day.

top **In Tomberg station a background of azure blue tiles is marked with abstract doodles based on the letters of the alphabet, which take on the appearance of imaginary creatures and objects.**

right **"Transcendence Platform" by Raoul Servais and Pierre Vlerickin at Houba–Brugmann station features a series of freeze-frame images – one set of a young woman jumping, another of a group of people standing.**

munich

Construction of the Munich subway, better know as the U-Bahn, began in1965 and the first two lines were completed by the end of 1971 in readiness for the city's hosting of the 1972 Olympic Games. The U-Bahn was originally planned with only 12km (7½ miles) of track, 13 stations, and just two lines. Since then it has expanded rapidly into a 79km (49-mile) network with 80 stations and six lines that are used by 288 million passengers every year.

The Munich subway called for not only innovative technological solutions and state-of-the-art tunnel engineering, but also architecture of the very highest standards. From start to finish the clarity, coherence, and aesthetic of station designs present a seamless architecture that relies on understatement, expression of construction detail, and the subtle play between harmony and contrast.

When taking a ride on the Munich subway the attentive passenger will notice that the station designers were not only concerned with the functionality of the structures for handling passenger flow or with the durability of the materials, but that they also focused their attention toward a contemporary appearance, to the visual quality of the public spaces. A journey through the network mirrors the changing tastes and architectural styles of more than 30 years of subway history.

Some may see the architecture of the 1970s stations as restrained, sober, and functional – characteristic of the Bauhaus movement. The 1971 Munchener Freiheit station on the U6 line, for example, typifies the clean lines and unadorned bare surfaces of Modernism, relying on the scale and proportioning of the internal space for expression, with massive square concrete columns rising through the platform floors. When the surface patina of dirt accumulated over the decades meant that the station had to be refurbished, previously bare columns were covered with pleasing blue tiles and the internal lighting of the platforms increased to dispel any gloomy corners, but otherwise its character was left untouched.

Later stations built in the 1980s and early 1990s are more eclectic, with curved lines,

above, left **The walls of the station of Candidplatz are clad in coloured metal panels arranged in a cadence of changing hues of reds, greens, and yellows. The bright yet diffuse ceiling light bathes the platform and tops of the columns suggesting sunshine streaming in.**

above, right **The cut and cover station box at Josephsburg has a crisp, flat, metal-clad ceiling canopy and an understated yet effective red colouring on the wall panels.**

right **The shimmering canopy of angled aluminium slats throws remarkable shadows over the walls of Grosshadern station. The walls are murals of geological strata, finely grained and exquisitely composed.**

left **The curved glass of the street level canopy of St Quirin–Platz sweeps down to meet the contiguous piled wall of the station at platform level. This is an audacious and innovative design that exploits the slope of the site to bring natural light deep into the station.**

coloured cladding panels to ensure dirt-free surfaces, dramatic lighting effects, and the use of enamelled and multicoloured glass. One of the most innovative designs for the extended section of the U6 to the west was for Grosshadern station, which opened in 1993. The long rectangular platform hall has a streamlined and profiled metal ceiling supported by a central row of cylindrical columns clad in bright yellow enamelled sheeting, enhancing the visual appeal of both surfaces. The walls of concrete on either side of the island platform have been painted in soft earth colours

to portray the geological strata of gravel, silt, clay, and rock that was excavated – their subtle hues glazed onto the walls are a joy to behold. The intelligent use of lighting above the canopied ceiling adds to the sensory delight, at the same time throwing an even spread of light onto the painted platform walls and shiny central columns.

Occasionally architecture accomplishes something that we might say is close to perfection in conveying a unity and an overwhelming sense of good order. The Munich U-Bahn is such an architecture.

right This extravagant ceiling dominates the platform of Hasenbergl station. It is a three-dimensional canopy screen intended to resemble the leaf of a rubber tree plant, and hangs from steel cables attached to the concrete roof slab. The vaulted profile of the surface is iridescent under artificial lighting.

bottom Messestadt station offers a contrast to Hasenbergl (above) – the restraint and plain-walled decoration of the simple box structure holds a deeper resonance of integrity, more reliant upon constructive honesty than cosmetic overkill. The hollowed recesses in the roof bring light to the platform and there are no fussy attachments to disturb the harmony.

right At Westfriedhof a string of large protruding ceiling lights becomes the dominant feature of the station. Each giant lampshade is lit with a different coloured lamp, creating a captivating visual stream.

station art and architecture

line a, prague

When you go down to the platforms on Line A of the Prague metro, take sunglasses and prepare to be stunned. The walls have a dazzling, pulsating skin like the glazed hide of a giant armadillo or a dalek's epidermis. In hues of blue, azure, maroon, green, amber, coffee and biscuit, they are embellished with rows of shiny, saucer-shaped metal motifs – some protruding like pimples, some indented like pockmarks – that tease and tantalize the eye.

Is this a homage to the kinetic art of Victor Vasarely, the mobile sculptures of Alexander Calder, the moiré lines of Bridget Riley, or the rhythmic squares of Josef Albers? The reference to optical and kinetic art of the 1970s certainly seems unmistakable, as does the link with the high-tech architecture of machine-made design. The light falling on the indented and protruding saucer shapes creates interference patterns that cause the eye to see shadows, sometimes behind, sometimes in front of them, making them appear to float. There is a feeling of movement and altered perspective that creates a sensation of acute dynamism even for the stationary observer.

Whatever the influences may have been, Prague must be commended for such a bold and audacious design. It would be fitting to pay tribute to the artists and architects who collaborated on the design of Line A stations but their names are not public knowledge. All we know is that the overall design and architecture of the metro was managed by Dr Otruba of the Design Centre, a department within the Transportation Board. Outside companies were called in to help, as the volume of work could not be handled by the Design Centre in the time that was allocated. The Military Design Institute provided the specification and documentation for the interiors of three stations, another company – Hydroprojects – designed two stations, while the rest were dealt with by the Design Centre.

What distinguishes Prague from other metro stations is the development of a unifying architectural style that is both distinctive and timeless in conception yet simple and cost-effective in its execution. A successful metro has to respond to many different and conflicting demands put upon it: it must be a dynamic part

above **Hradcanska station on Line A with its mesmerizing dimpled panels on a background of rich tonal colours defies classification. Although created with a limited budget, this station shows how great architecture can transform the mundane into the sublime.**

of the city's transportation system, harmonize
with the built environment, maintain a clear
identity, and have the flexibility to adapt to
increases in passenger numbers in the future,
which are never easy to predict.

Added to these demands that affect metros
the world over were Prague's specific political
pressures, financial constraints, shortage (at the
time) of durable stone for covering the walls,
and lack of local construction experience in
building an underground railway. But the team
were fast learners. As part of the design
philosophy, the stations of Line A have their
ceilings clad in the same pale bronze panels
throughout, while the curving walls down the
sides are set in different colours to distinguish
one station wall from another. The dimpled and
flat panels are made from pressed aluminium
sheeting with the colours enamelled on. The
wall colour graduates in shade as it reaches
platform level. Standardizing the panel sizes
has significantly reduced their maintenance and
replacement costs.

The metro network of Prague is served by
three main lines that criss-cross the city in a
triangle. The first line – rather confusingly, it
called Line C – runs north to south and is
14.2km (8¾ miles) long. It was opened in 1974,
then extended further south in 1980, and four
years later crossed the River Vltava that divides
the city. The east–west Line A was opened in
1978 and continued to be developed until 1990.
It has a track length of 9.9km (just over 6 miles)
with 12 stations that run from Skalka in the east
to Dejvicka in the west. The newest line is Line B,
which opened in 1985 and has a track length of
25.8km (16 miles).

right A close-up of the
very tactile panels that
line the walls of Line A
stations, with the acoustic
dampers in between
(Prague boasts the best
acoustics of any metro).
This is the wall of Muzeum
interchange station.

below Vysocanska station
on Line B was constructed
in 1998. Although it is
considerably more recent
than the Line A stations, it
feels less modern.

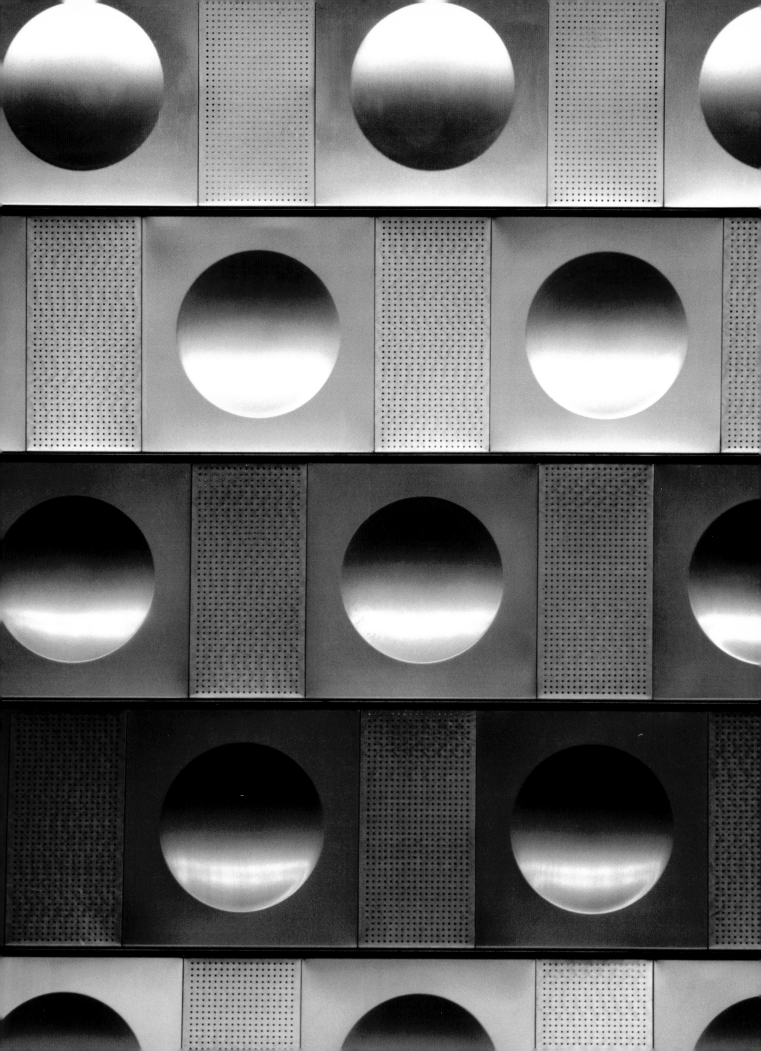

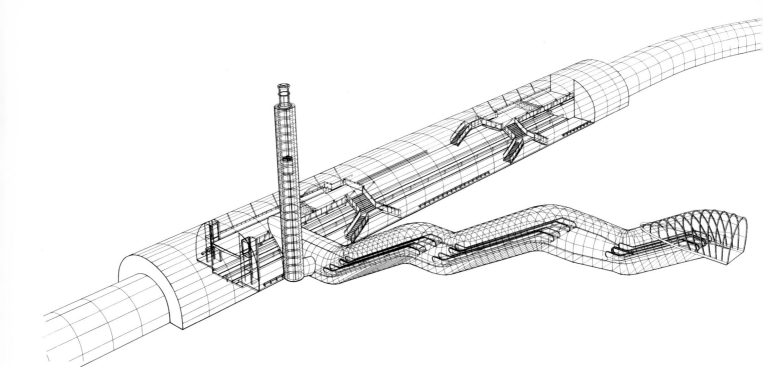

bilbao

The metropolitan area of Bilbao has developed linearly along both banks of the river estuary that divides the city. At the upper end, where the river narrows, the two halves of the city meet to become the centre of Bilbao and the business district. The route of the Bilbao metro can be represented by the letter Y. The left arm of the Y is served by Line 1 with 27 stations that run along the left bank and through the residential districts, the first phase of which was complete in 1995. Line 2, which runs along the right bank and is 20km (12½ miles) long, was opened in 2002. The top end of both lines merge and continue into the city centre over 10.5km (6½ miles) of track. The metro trains link coastal villages, the industrial zones, the suburbs, and the city centre, providing a high-quality service for more than one million

people. The architects Norman Foster and Partners, who were responsible for designing the first eight stations on Line 1 made these comments about their design approach:

An underground system ... can rapidly degenerate into a confusing, ill-maintained, and potentially dangerous labyrinth. The guiding principle behind our design proposals for the new Bilbao subway was the need to strip the problem down to its essentials. At street level, the metro is announced by curved glass enclosures, which admit natural light by day and are illuminated by night. Below, the 16-metre-wide station caverns, which form the heart of the system, are reached as simply and directly as possible by escalators and glass lifts. The cavern form, which is a direct engineered response to the forces of nature, is celebrated rather than disguised in the design of the station. The lightweight and maintenance-free, prefabricated components (mezzanines, stairs, ticket barriers, and lifts) are treated as separate elements and make a strong contrast with the precast concrete walls of the cavern. Ventilation ducts and electrical cables are hidden from view and run below the platforms.

right **The view from platform level looking up to the elevated central mezzanine walkway.**

station art and architecture

left **An axonometric projection of a typical Bilbao metro station showing the entrance canopy and escalators leading down to the tunnelled platform shell.**

The Bilbao metro was conceived as a total architecture with a repeating rhythm of platform spaces and canopied entrances to make the metro structure friendly and recognizable. The curved glass canopy entrances to the stations, nicknamed "fosteritos" by the locals, make visible landmarks on the streetscape with their tunnel shapes protruding from the building line. The light-filled entrances are a welcoming sign and a beacon by night for ease of identification. They have become emblematic of the Bilbao metro in much the same way as are the Art Nouveau entrances of the early Paris Métro.

An underground system is often conceived as a series of station boxes connected by tunnels, where the train journey is seen in isolation to the spaces for the people even though the experience of travel is a single event, that starts and ends at street level. The stations, the escalators, and the platforms for the Bilbao metro were designed to emphasize the unity of its appearance throughout, exploiting the wider internal spaces generated by the technical engineering of its construction. The expertise of Spanish engineers in using mobile gantries for the aerospace industry was called into play to place the prefabricated concrete lining panels of the tunnelled station enclosures. The bare, raw energy of the simple yet curving concrete structure liberates the space and is in direct contrast to other stations where the walls are vertical and the ceilings flat, which tends to confine space.

above **The only obvious difference between the stations on the Bilbao metro is their names; everything else is exactly the same – colour, walkways, internal construction, and signage.**

below **The suspended mezzanine walkway bridging the tracks gives access to both platforms and to the exit barriers. The walls of the tunnels are dressed in buff precast concrete panels.**

right **Another view of the mezzanine walkway that takes passengers to the platform levels, this time down the escalator banks.**

station art and architecture

jubilee line extension, london

Roland Paoletti was brought over from Hong Kong, where he had been chief architect for the Mass Transit Railway, to develop the architectural concept for the whole of the Jubilee Line Extension. Given his Hong Kong experience, it was firmly expected that he would create a unified design theme for all the stations, based on conventional engineering solutions. But Paoletti had other ideas, proposing that each of the 11 stations from Westminster to Stratford in East London would be designed as an individual entity, linked to the others by an underlying philosophy. Each should be unique and should contribute strongly to its neighbourhood. Some stations – such as Canary Wharf, Westminster, and North Greenwich – would have more money spent on them than others. Certainly, the above-ground stations – with the exception of Canning Town, where complex engineering problems had to be overcome because of a light rail overhead – had a minuscule architectural budget to work with by comparison.

A different London architect was chosen for each station. There were practical reasons for spreading the load. One architect would have found it difficult to achieve the quality and the deliberate variation in style between stations that Paoletti was searching for, particularly given the short time that was available to produce drawings for construction. No one was selected on reputation alone: like-minded architects were chosen, who, it was thought, would fulfill the brief well and who possessed the necessary understanding of the engineering requirements.

The design priorities were to provide a generous and easily understood space, clear and direct passenger routing, a sufficiency of escalators, elevators for the disabled, and safety in all aspects, particularly in the provision of protected escape routes. As a feature of all the stations, Paoletti wanted the civil engineering to be exposed wherever possible.

This open-minded commissioning policy, giving some of the country's best architects free

far left **The form of the building of Stratford station is expressed as a curved roof springing from an upper level walkway, geometrically defined as a sector of a circle. Architect: Wilkinson Eyre.**

left **The construction elements of the structure of Ian Ritchie's Bermondsey station are expressed clearly and seamlessly. Seen here is the escalator shaft leading to the platforms.**

below **The use of natural light and a minimalist structure brings a sensitivity to Bermondsey station's ticket hall.**

bottom **Foster and Partners' Canary Wharf, the cathedral of light. This is architectural engineering of the highest integrity, whose pure form creates dramatic vistas like this view of the entrance canopy and escalators seen from the ticket hall.**

left and below **The beautiful glass rotunda of the entrance hall to Canada Water station is a modern twist to Holden's Arnos Grove on the Piccadilly Line Extension and an architecture of inspiring creativity. Architect: JLE Architects.**

right **Architects Weston Williamson created snaking reticulated walls of cast iron for London Bridge station. Stove enamelled panels graduate in colour from deep blue at the base to pale grey over the ceiling, where they are perforated for acoustic damping.**

ordinary as the tail end of an existing tube line. What the extension managed to do was to allow heavy engineering, which is so often static and inhuman, to become instead resourceful and brilliant and active in response to architectural initiatives.

The JLE stations of Canary Wharf, Bermondsey, London Bridge, and Stratford are worth particular attention because they capture the best in architectural endeavour of three generic station types – the deep tunnel station, the cut and cover box, and the ground-level platform. Of these, Canary Wharf perhaps ranks highest in terms of its organization of internal space – the excess clutter of services and ticket counters are tucked neatly along the sides of the ticket hall. From platform level up to the ticket hall daylight filters down the vast open corridors leading you skyward.

Bermondsey is also a jewel among all the underground stations, and should be the template for the design of all cut and cover stations. Although constrained by cost and the confinement of space, engineering and aesthetic have become one expression through refinement of structural form and the subtlety of detailing.

At the eastern end of the extension is the stunning glass-clad enclosure of Stratford station. The lightweight truss, standing 8m (26ft) high and spanning the length of the building supported on four precast columns, is a work of engineering art. So, too, is the wonderful sweep of the silky smooth canopy roof and the crisply detailed connection of steelwork, holding-down bolts, and foundation plinth visible on the high-level walkway.

rein to challenge civil engineering preconceptions and allowing them to work on stations in their entirety from street to platform level, was rewarded with a highly functional series of bold and intelligent station designs.

When Paoletti was asked about the achievements of the JLE, he stated:

It is impossible to imagine two more inflexible cultures than those of heavy railways and infrastructural engineering. An underground railway has both. The JLE's extraordinary achievement has been to break with a tradition of design conformity, developed and consolidated for over a century, and create something of exceptional quality from something as

overleaf **The glass filigree structure of Stratford station is a beacon by night. The curved canopy roof cantilevering from its base is a lightweight parasol of minimal thickness.**

right **The luminous double-height space for the Line 14 platform at Gare de Lyon. With its glass-walled elevators and overhead walkways it looks more like a covered shopping mall than a metro station.**

below, left **Gare de Lyon interchange station and the new escalators leading to the Line 14 platforms.**

line 14, paris

In 1998 the first new Métro line for over 60 years was opened in Paris. Line 14, also known as the Météor Line (Métro Est–Ouest Rapide), runs from Madeleine to Saint-Lazare via Pyramides, Châtelet, Gare de Lyon, Bercy, and Cour St-Emilion in 12 minutes. But this was more than just a new Métro line: it introduced a new train control system planned to revolutionize the network as a whole. The high-capacity, driverless trains have automatic guidance controls, allowing them to speed through Line 14 at two-minute intervals, transporting up to 40,000 passengers per hour. This is twice as many trains per hour and twice as many passengers as the regular Métro trains currently carry on other lines. The RATP, who run the network, plan to upgrade all the other lines with the new guidance system and driverless trains and double the line-wide capacity over the next decade.

Something new has also happened on Line 14 with regard to station design and architecture. Unlike the spartan designs of earlier Paris Métro stations, those on Line 14 are brightly lit,

spacious, engagingly uplifting and fabulous to look at. What has caused the shift in design philosophy? Architects Bernard Kohn and Jean Pierre Vaysse, who between them designed six of the seven stations, explain:

We insisted on comprehensible, well-organized spaces that that as a whole would contribute to the public grasp of the stations. A civil engineer once told us, "we are the diggers; you guys stick to the architectural features". Yet we have always striven to think of the project as not a box in which the architect is merely the decorator but rather is the designer of the whole. One of the major issues was making the structure of the stations visible and legible, in accordance with a basic ethical principle: the project is designed for the public, from whom we have nothing to hide. Instead of creating circulation paths that arrived at platform level, we opted for mezzanines from which people can look down on the platforms before descending to them.

This is not to say that earlier stations on other lines that have since been refurbished are devoid of artistic or architectural merit. On the contrary, there are a number of stations – such as Chessy and Villejuif Leo Lagrange, for example – that have printed graphic art work on their walls. But none was conceived as part of the original construction and there are few such stations on any one line. The Météor Line is unique in that its stations are not merely decorated boxes but rather present a holistic architecture of great visual quality.

below **The refurbishment of Cité station on Line 4 shows that architectural achievement on the Métro has not been limited to the new Line 14 stations. Cité now has a wonderful elevated walkway that leads down to the platforms, better visibility, poster-free walls, and lighting that is in keeping with its original design.**

right, top **The unique cradling framework over the tracks of Line 14 supports the safety screen wall on the platform edge. Here, two driverless automatic trains are stopping at Châtelet station.**

right, bottom **Looking down the escalator to the platform of Line 14 at Gare de Lyon. The shallow below-ground station overlooks a colonnaded atrium on one side, which is open to natural light and a cheerful patch of greenery.**

line 14, paris 113

north east line, singapore

The new North East Line is the flagship of Singapore's Mass Rapid Transit, with station architecture and train technology that is considered to be of world-class standing. The MRT opened in 1987 with a network length of 83km (51½ miles), operating six-car trains, all fully air conditioned and carrying a maximum of 320 persons per train at peak times. In June 2002 the North East Line opened with 16 architecturally designed stations covering 20km (12½ miles) and operating the world's first fully automatic, pantograph underground railway powered by overhead high-voltage cable. This is unlike the rest of the system, which is powered by a third rail. Together with the 6km (3¾-mile) Changi Airport extension and the recently opened Sengkang Light Rapid Transit link, the NEL extends the MRT network from 83km (51½ miles) with 58 stations in the 1990s to 121km (75 miles) with 85 stations today.

The Land Transport Authority, who are responsible for running the SMRT, adopted an approach to the station design and architecture on the NEL that was to incorporate clear signage and route direction, spaciousness and visibility with double-height central atrium spaces, and integration with other transport modes. Every station was to have a unique identity, with art work on the walls and barrier-free facilities for the disabled. Wherever possible, the underground stations were to be linked to commercial developments, with underpass crossings at street level to enter the system.

Reducing congestion at peak times was of vital importance in the layout and planning of the stations. A way of allowing the greatest amount of space for passenger movement to and from the platforms was required. Comparative studies were carried out to evaluate the merits and pitfalls of island platforms and side platform stations. On balance, the island platforms offered better long-term maintenance and operational advantages than the side platforms. It was more convenient for passengers to move across a platform to choose a train in either direction, and the need for duplicate escalators and staircases was eliminated.

The characteristic wide corridors of the MRT stations derive from the need to evacuate passengers in an emergency from the remotest point on the platform to a point of safety above ground in less than six minutes. The stations have been designed to meet the stringent requirements of current American fire and safety codes. These determine to a great extent the number, location, and widths of staircases, escalators, and ticket barriers, and the length of travel from platform to concourse. Comfort is

left **Located next to the People's Park in Singapore, this tall glass-panelled pagoda structure heralds the entrance to Chinatown station, which reflects the rich oriental culture and vibrancy of the area.**

below **Punggol**, one of only two above-ground stations on the North East Line, is also the longest station of the network, measuring 320m (1,050ft). This futuristic structure is enclosed in aluminium, which opens skyward to allow daylight in.

bottom With its close proximity to the sea front, it is fitting that the **Harbour Front** station has a nautical theme, with soothing blue walls, sailing motifs, and an escalator well of bright metal balustrades fashioned in the style of modern cruise ships.

right The bright panelling of the structural surfaces and a colourful mural running along the circumference of the light-well above platform level give a lightness of touch to **Buangkok** station.

below, right **Chinatown** entrance concourse has a resplendent mural designed by Tan Swie Hian. Titled "The Phoenix Eye's Domain", it symbolizes the migration of early Chinese settlers to Singapore.

far left **The cool depths of the Dhoby Ghaut station, one of finest architectural stations on the network. Smooth sheets of glass enclose the staircases and balustrades, while enamelled metal panels caress the arched walkways and ceilings.**

left **The expansive and luminous entrance hall to Sengkang station continues the "house style" of smooth shiny panelling on walls and columns. Nevertheless, each station on the line retains its own architectural identity.**

also a consideration: as well as serving as a safety barrier, platform screen doors prevent conditioned cool air from within the station escaping into the tunnel, thus maintaining a pleasant temperature on the platforms.

Construction of the North East Line spanned six years from 1997 to 2002 and involved tunnelling under some of Singapore's oldest buildings and cutting open the middle of busy roads in heavily built-up areas, to serve new towns and expanding commercial districts. The new NEL, with a station architecture that in many ways echoes some of the grandeur of the Moscow metro, gives commuters and visitors to Singapore a fast, comfortable, and enjoyable journey into the city centre, reminding them of the benefits of a progressive country and a dynamic economy.

sheppard subway, toronto

Despite the many remarkable engineering feats involved in the construction of Toronto's Sheppard Subway – it used enough concrete to construct six CN Towers, for example – the public acclaim that greeted its opening on 22 November 2002 was mostly generated by the rich and stimulating art work that covers the walls, ceilings, and platforms of all five stations.

When you enter a station on the Sheppard Subway you walk into a total art experience. Artists have created imaginative environments in each of the stations, expressing themes of community, location, and heritage. The work of 300 artists from across the state of Ontario was reviewed during an open competition and then this number was whittled down to six. The winning artists were selected for their experience with public commissions, their understanding of the materials and process of their art, and for their ability to work with architects and engineers as part of the design team. The art that was transferred to the station fabric is made of durable, low-maintenance materials that are resistant to vandalism, generally ceramic wall tiles and terrazzo-type floor screeds.

Public art was seen by the Toronto Transit Commission as playing a significant role in the design of the new line, giving each station a meaningful identity within the local community. They have succeeded magnificently in their aim.

On the interior walls of Sheppard-Yonge station is the work of artist Stacey Spiegel. It is a panoramic landscape that expresses the rocks, fields, trees, water, and buildings you might see from the road on a compressed journey through southern Ontario. The images run continuously along the walls from one platform to the other. One hundred and fifty separate photographic images were taken, digitized, and blended using computer technology to create the 1.5 million mosaic tiles that cover the walls.

The walls of Bayview station are splashed with bold, playful doodles by Panya Clark Espinal. They depict everyday objects and simple recognizable geometric shapes on an uncommonly large scale. When seen from a distance the shapes are identifiable, but as you pass close by them they deconstruct to become an abstract design.

Sylvie Belanger, on the other hand, has taken photographic images of people who travel on the subway and has reconstructed them as large tile friezes on the walls of Bessarion station. Some images emphasize folded hands, others a collection of feet, or the backs of people's heads. Her work forms an essay on the different ages, genders, races, and social groups that use the subway.

At Leslie station, artist Micah Lexier has sampled the handwriting of 3,400 different people, including local residents, school children, subway passengers, and metro employees. The title of the work, "Ampersand", is derived from the symbol that links the same two handwritten words that appear on every tile.

The wall tiles by Stephen Cruise at Don Mills station record the actual fossils and other objects uncovered during the excavation of the line. Other walls feature images of local flora and fauna, and the terrazzo floor tiles are embellished with the outline of terrapin shells.

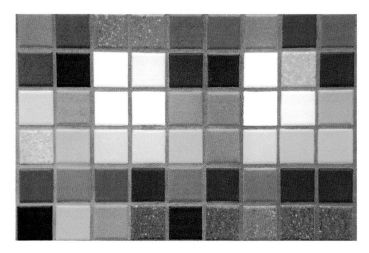

left and below **Artist Sylvie Belanger** has used photographs of people using the subway at Bessarion station to create a vivid and personalized montage of heads, hands, and feet imprinted on ceramic wall tiles.

right, top and bottom **One of the most imaginative and interactive works of art on the Sheppard Subway is at Bayview station. Panya Clark Espinal's bold, whimsical, larger-than-life images of familiar objects are stretched and distorted to flow from the walls onto the platform floors.**

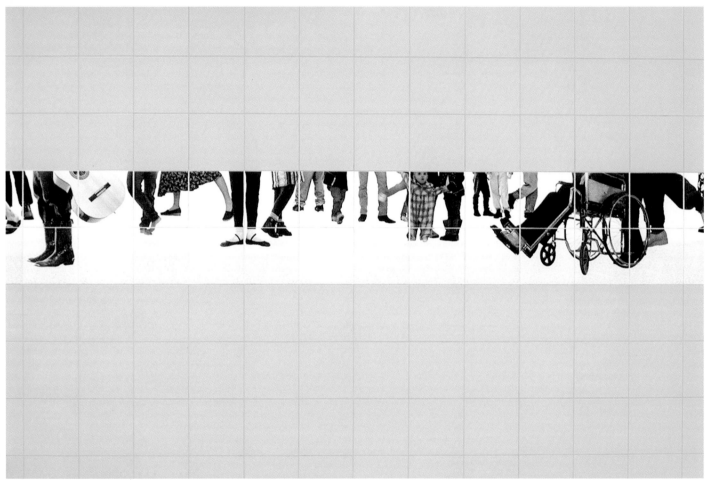

left **The MTR symbol at the entrance to Tung Chung station on Lantau Island. The attached high-rise development, linked with station and built at the same time, is also under MTR ownership.**

below **The Operation Control Centre is the heart of the MTR network and controls all six lines, which run on mainland Kowloon and across to Hong Kong and Lantau islands.**

hong kong

Established in 1976, the Hong Kong Mass Transit Railway is, in every way, the most up-to-date metro system in the world, with an overall network length of 87.7km (54½ miles) served by six lines. Of the 49 stations, 33 are located underground and vary in depth from 12m (40ft) to 37m (121ft) below street level. The construction of these underground stations ranges from simple box structures, with concourse and platforms on two and three levels, to complex layouts with platforms in bored tunnels and off-street concourse structures housing basements of up to seven floors below the street.

With a daily patronage of more than 2.3 million passengers, the Hong Kong MTR is one of the most intensively used networks in the world. It provides 19 hours of passenger service daily, running from 6am through to 1am the following morning.

The fast Airport Express Line opened in 1998, linking Hong Kong International Airport with the urban centres of Tung Chung, Tsing Yi, and Hong Kong. The line covers the 35.3km (22 mile) journey in 23 minutes. For the first time on an MTR line, these new stations included specially commissioned art work integrated into the architecture with the aim of creating a more interesting travelling environment and making passenger journeys more enjoyable. Meanwhile, the current modernization programme to upgrade older stations has also introduced art work as part of the improvements.

station art and architecture

top left **This mural is by artist Chu Hung. It is located at Yau Ma Tei station and titled "My Home".**

top right **The first metro stations in Hong Kong were simple box structures, like this one, whose walls were covered in single-colour tiles throughout, using – typically – greens, reds, and yellows.**

above **Art has been integrated into the latest stations of the MTR to make passenger journeys more enjoyable. Artist Freeman Lau has created colourful suspended mobiles titled "Links" at Tung Chung Station.**

red line, los angeles

The Los Angeles County Metropolitan Authority (MTA) serves as a transportation provider and operator for one of the largest counties in the state of California. More than 9.6 million people live, work, and play within its 3,711sq km (1,433sq mile) service zone. Besides operating more than 2,000 peak-hour buses on an average weekday, it runs 96.5 route kilometres (60 route miles) of a metro rail service. There are three lines – the Metro Red Line, Metro Blue Line, and Metro Green Line – which consist of more than 50 stations along a network that stretches from Long Beach to Downtown LA and on to Hollywood; from Universal City and North Hollywood in the San Fernando Valley to Norwalk and El Segundo.

As expansion and improvements continue to fully integrate the city transit systems – buses, smart shuttles, light rail, the subway, carpool lanes, and bikeways – the future means more transportation choices for those who live and work in the Los Angeles area. The Metro Blue Line opened in 1990, the Green Line in 1995, and the architecturally eclectic Red Line, which started in 1993, has just added the cinematic North Hollywood Line stations to the network.

The Red Line has 16 stations, which are located in business districts and feature unique public works of art. The stations are linked by twin tunnels with special facilities to allow filming in the stations and tunnels.

At Pershing Square station on the Red Line, located on Hill Street in downtown LA, the neon lighting suspended from the ceiling in whirls of pink and blue makes spectacular reflections on the roof and walls of the station. At Westlake/Macarthur Park, a powerfully symbolic mural in richly coloured hues by Francisco Letelier straddles the staircase leading down to the platform. Hollywood/Highland station on the North Hollywood extension of the Red Line is the stop for the Kodak Theatre, where the Academy Awards Ceremony takes place, along other spectacular events. The station's highly stylized steelwork supports and overhead lighting canopy evoke the bright lights of tinsel town, giving a flavour of glitz and glamour. At Hollywood/Vine, you enter a fantasy oasis of gaudy orange columns with fake metal palms reaching into an artificial night sky covered in strips of actual cine film to provide a

shimmering, star-spangled backdrop. The platforms seats are decorated with pictures of limousines of the roaring '40s. The theme of North Hollywood station at the end the Red Line is "The California Dream", to celebrate and honour the generations of immigrants who came to the area with great hope and dreams of a better future. Artist Anne Maries Karlsen created a series of colourful murals on the station walls that appear to the viewer as though he or she is looking through a kaleidoscope.

Recognizing that art can bring a touch of humanity to an often dull train journey, the MTA commissions artists to incorporate art in a wide variety of transportation projects. From bus stops to rail stations, from bus interiors to barrier fences, poetry, graphic design, and art work create a sense of place and engage the travelling public. This was critical to Metro Rail, which was only introduced to the city ten years ago and

needed good promotional ideas to attract new customers. The Metro Art Department of the MTA, which was established in 1989 for just this purpose, has commissioned more than 250 works of art, which are on permanent and temporary display throughout the transport network. Such has been the success of the programme and its community involvement that it has been recognized as the most imaginative arts programme in the country.

The MTA spend half a per cent of the construction cost of any new undertaking on art and station enhancement, not a trifling sum when the budget runs into several hundred million dollars. Architects and artists are brought together as design teams to let their imagination build these subterranean theatres of dreams within the coffers of a subway structure – a picture palace, a garden of delight, an oasis of fantasy, an illuminated pleasure land – pure Hollywood… what else!

left **Lighting designer and artist Stephen Antonakas has created a wonderland of dazzling, twisting, looping neon tube lights suspended from the high ceiling that runs the length of the platform at Pershing Square station.**

above **At Hollywood/ Highland, artist Sheila Klein and architects Dworsky Associates have brought sculptural art playfully into the platform enclosure. Stylized metal casing and finials attach themselves like ivy around the central columns, a framework of curved metal ribs tied to the columns appear to prop up the translucent glass of the ceiling light while acting as a hanger for signage to the platforms below.**

underground culture

tickets

It's no use expanding the underground network and increasing train frequency without improving passenger circulation and flow at the busy stations. The automatic ticket barrier is a clever piece of mechanical engineering that makes for a quick entry and exit, allowing tickets with magnetic strips or a smart card to open the gates.

Most modern metro stations now have automatic ticket barriers, the type and number depending largely on the peak flow of passengers, but there are still a few exceptions. On the Hamburg metro, for example, you can just walk through the open gates to get to your train – though many inspectors patrol the carriages, and not having a ticket can lead to a hefty fine.

More and more metro authorities are encouraging their customers to purchase smart cards, which look like credit cards and only have to be swiped over the electric eye processor at the entry and exit to open the barriers.

Unlike many other authorities, the Sapporo City Transportation Bureau in Japan has different ticket face designs to make the various ticket types easy to identify, as well as attractive to look at. They even offer made-to-order cards, enabling passengers to print their own design on the card face, and cards intended to be given as gifts, which have beautiful flower pictures on them. The cards are so attractive that some people have started collecting them as mementos.

top left and right **The new smart cards are like credit cards that are swiped over the ticket barriers and recharged at vending machines. The one on the left is for Singapore metro; top right is a Washington metro card.**

right **These sleek automatic ticket barriers are at Harbour Front station on the Singapore MTR.**

underground culture

below **A selection of cards for the Sapporo metro. From top left: eco ticket for subway, bus, and streetcar; day-time discount coupon; card with set value; one-day travel card; one-day card for travel on buses, subway, and streetcars; rechargeable smart card.**

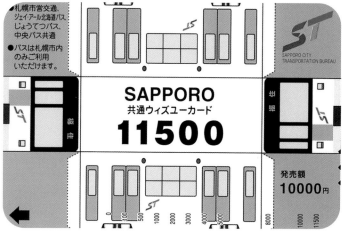

poster art

The underground and elevated metro networks were built to whisk commuters quickly and efficiently into the heart of the city and out again. The number of carriages, the frequency of trains, and the capacity of the system was geared to cater for the rush hour – those peak times between 7am and 10am and from 4pm to 7pm on week days. Outside of these times trains often ran quite empty. In addition to reducing the frequency of trains, operators of the underground looked for ways to increase weekend and off-peak travel by selling cheaper tickets and encouraging trips to the countryside or local attractions.

The mainline railways were already hard at work at the turn of the 20th century promoting leisure travel with colourful posters and booklets showing off the delights of exhilarating scenery to be enjoyed in far-away places. In the USA it was a trip to the Niagara Falls, the Grand Canyon, the Rocky Mountains, Yellowstone Park, or the St Louis Bridge and the mighty Mississippi. The underground network could not compete with the distances covered by the mainline railways, but there was a wealth of local attractions close to the city centres it could take people to – museums, art galleries, exhibition centres, amusement parks, sporting events, and theatres. So they focused their attention on publicizing these places.

In 1908 London Underground started a campaign to design and publish its own advertising material to promote leisure travel at off-peak times. By the middle of the 1920s they were so successful with their campaign that they had surpassed the efforts of their much larger mainline rivals in the field of poster promotion. The phenomenal success of the underground

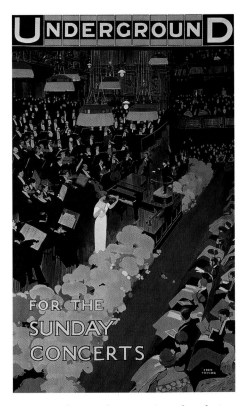

poster was down to the enterprise and marketing skills of one man in particular, Frank Pick. He was a solicitor by training, who joined London Underground in 1908 as their publicity manager and set about commissioning posters designed by some of the best artists in the country. By 1938, following the introduction of cheap off-peak travel tickets and the arrival of large department stores, leisure travel on the underground was bringing in a lot of revenue.

Pick planned various poster campaigns and adopted particular styles that would be displayed on the underground stations, the trams, and

below, left **A poster designed by Fred Taylor in 1912 to promote underground travel to the concert halls of London in the evenings.**

right **Captivating images suggested the idea of travel without the need for printed information. This was Clive Gardner's cubist interpretation of the Palm House in Kew Gardens, London, issued in 1926.**

THE PALM HOUSE
KEW GARDENS
BUT SEE IT FOR YOURSELF

BY UNDERGROUND TO
KEW GARDENS
STATION

JOHNSON, RIDDLE & CO., LTD., LONDON, S.E.I

above **Images of special shopping trips were targeted at women to encourage off-peak travel. Horace Tailor's poster "To The Summer Sales" was issued in 1926.**

top **Promoting sporting events was a major boost for subway travel during off-peak times. This poster titled "Epsom Summer Meeting" was designed by Sybil Andrews and Cyril Power in 1933, but is signed Andrew Power – a composite of their surnames.**

above **A poster by internationally known artist Zero, whose real name was Hans Schleger, enriched the range of London Underground poster art in 1935.**

the countryside farther away from London. It is almost impossible today to imagine Hounslow Heath or Perivale as pleasant, leafy countryside villages. The former is now Heathrow Airport and the latter is part of a large industrial estate in West London adjacent to the M40 corridor.

Underground poster art was a very English phenomenon – nowhere else in the world has art and graphic design of such quality been used to promote travel on the underground. By the 1960s, with so many people using the underground during off-peak times, the "Go By Underground Poster" in London was replaced by more esoteric ones explaining what the subway company was doing to improve travel on the overcrowded system.

Quite a number of metro authorities today run poster campaigns and poster design competitions to promote awareness of safety on the subway. The Washington metro, for example, holds an annual student poster contest on safety issues that is open to any young person from elementary, middle, or high school in the metro region. It also runs advertisements in the local newspapers under the theme of "open doors" to help its customers find jobs, make career improvements, get better education, and to encourage them to participate in the region's rich cultural and entertainment programmes. In 1968 posters and car stickers were printed in their thousands to make people aware of the need for local funding through revenue bonds to secure the construction budget for building the Washington metro. A full-scale mock-up of the metro railcar was exhibited on the lawns of the White House and then shown at shopping malls around the area to generate interest in and public support for the metro.

trolley buses. The promotion campaign would coincide with a number of seasonal attractions throughout the year, including Wimbledon week, the Boat Race, cricket at Lords, the FA Cup Final, motor shows, winter and summer sales, Trooping the Colour, and so on. And at all times travellers were reminded of the attractions of the countryside, the fresh air, and open spaces that the underground network could reach, enticing city dwellers keen to escape the urban grime to take the tube to Kew Gardens, Richmond Park, Hainault Forest, or Ealing Common. Ironically, by the 1960s the underground system itself was indirectly responsible for the demise of much of the countryside. Wherever a new line was built and new stations had opened, building mushroomed and residential areas grew, pushing

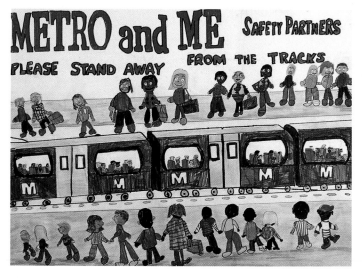

graffiti art

Daubed and scrawled doodles, cartoons, and messages on trains, station walls, and subways have been a trait of the underground ever since the invention of the aerosol can. Understandably, the attitude of railway authorities is negative: graffiti is one of the worst forms of pollution that the subway system has to combat and costs millions of dollars every year to remove.

Yet many of the users of the subway – and even the transport authorities – have noticed that certain "graffiti" is tolerable, because of the quality of the art work and humour in the message. Recognition of graffiti as an art form in Barcelona, for example, has resulted in an entire station at Hostafrancs being decorated in tiles with graffiti motifs. Some metro stations in Brussels and the Netherlands have also been influenced by graffiti art in the way they have covered vast stretches of the station walls in strongly coloured abstract and surreal motifs.

Until a few years ago, a number of trains on the New York subway were never cleaned of their graffiti – they were so imaginatively designed that users of the subway system thought they were great to look at. The pen names of the best artists were often boldly sprayed on the graffiti and there was intense rivalry between gangs.

There is a saying – "getting up" – among graffiti artists, that signifies acceptance and recognition of a person's aerosol skills. It is not a question of how pretty or dramatic an image may be, but of how often and on how many trains the art can be seen. This differentiates the New York subway writer from those that cover walls and bridge parapets with sign writing. Poor writing and deficiencies in graphic skill are overlooked, so long as the work is seen regularly on trains along a particular route. Individuals with a talent for painting whole

above, right **A "cop" character, the scourge of the graffiti writers, painted by Skeme in 1982 on a train that runs the length of Manhattan along Broadway. Although common in the 1980s, subway graffiti was seldom photographed; these three images from a photo essay by Martha Cooper are rare.**

right **Whole-car graffiti sprayed by writers Paze and Fome with a dedication to Pancho and Anita.**

cars will always earn the respect of other writers – size does matter. A whole car blitz is worth more than a cartoon or signature over a door panel.

Form and style are really important to a writer – the more complex and extravagant the piece, the higher the esteem and greater the admiration. There must be originality in the design, a smooth flow of the letters and symbols, and brightness of colour. Drips, paint runs, or paint black spots are frowned upon and indicate lack of control and competence. There must also be an effective highlight painted around the edges of letters or symbols to make them stand out.

When asked to give a profile of a typical graffiti artist, graffiti squad officers in New York say that they are predominantly teenage boys living in the city, usually between the ages of 11 and 16. They are just as likely to be the sons of doctors, professors, senators, and well-educated families as from families living in the ghetto areas. The lack of adult graffiti writers can perhaps be explained by the fact that the law gets tough on persons over 16 years of age found vandalizing public property.

Graffiti removal is a slow and painstaking business. Between 1971 and 1974 the subway employees of New York had to sand and repaint entire trains by hand, a job that took four days per car, the efforts of 20 cleaners, and 1,800 dollars worth of paint. It was equivalent to a loss in revenue of 6,000 ticket sales per car.

Subway authorities worldwide try to eradicate graffiti from their stations and trains by regular cleaning and by applying protective coatings that prevent paint adhering to the surfaces. Subways such as New York's that have little art work in their stations and miles of bare retaining walls between them are a natural conduit and playground for the graffiti vandal. But the Stockholm metro, with its wonderful art on its station walls, still suffers the same amount of destructive graffiti as New York. There can be no defence for anyone recognizing graffiti as art under these circumstances.

underground culture

decorated trains

Advertising posters slapped unimaginatively across the sides of access corridors, escalator shafts, and station walls have been shunned by all but a few metro authorities. They can destroy the integrity of the station architecture and its visibility, assailing the senses with unwanted slogans as well as increasing debris and dirt.

Those that continue with such a tradition do so because it brings in much-needed advertising revenue. They may give assurances that the posters are fire retardant and that advertising standards will be maintained to ensure that what is printed is in good taste, but it is still defacement by any definition. Perhaps one of the worst subways for its voracious and uncontrolled use of advertising posters is the

London Underground. Some time ago, the underground stations of Tottenham Court Road, Oxford Circus, Leicester Square, and Charing Cross were refurbished and the station walls boldly covered with new, imaginative designs. The stations were a revelation – they were bright and cheerful, devoid of posters, and received much praise for their architecture. Now, the continuity and visibility of such delightful colour patterns and tile motifs has been lost behind a morass of gaudy advertising graffiti – row upon row, wall after wall has been pasted with paper. The excuse for this is that London Underground needs every penny it can get to keep the network operating. It seems a shame, however, to compromise the architecture in this way. Perhaps an alternative approach would be to display some great art and ask passengers for donations.

In 1998, as an alternative to wall-to-wall poster advertising, the RATP in Paris bedecked some trains with all-over commercial advertisements as they do on buses and taxis. Chocolate bars, sporting events, hi-fi equipment, holidays abroad, department stores, and branded drinks were emblazoned on the outside of the carriages. This approach had an immediate appeal because as the train moves, the advertisement moves with it, leaving the station walls free of poster graffiti. Moreover, the advertisements are fun to look at and create abstract patterns as the train passes by. For the World Cup, which was held in France that year, RATP cars were specially painted to promote the event. Surely this is a far better answer to the need to generate advertising revenue than plastering walls in commercial posters.

right **Whole-train advertising is far cleaner, safer, and more attractive than are posters on station walls, which the RATP have banned. Paris Métro trains can promote cosmetic products (top), for example, and major sporting events, such as the World Cup in France in 1994 (bottom), on trains running the length of the line.**

above **On the small Berlin U-Bahn trains all-over advertising can earn revenue, like this example carrying an advertisement for the Citibank Corporation.**

below **A diagram of Reno's endless conveyer staircase (left), c.1892. G.A. Wheeler's flat step design of the treads, c.1892 (middle). Seeberger's flat step escalator with passenger diverter (right).**

right **A modern escalator on the Singapore MTR with glass sidewalls to support the escalator belt (top left). Well-illuminated signage and escalator entrance into Highland station on the LA metro (top right). Cut-away diagram showing working parts and framework of a modern escalator (bottom).**

escalators

If the elevator had not been invented we would not have skyscrapers or deep underground stations. But while elevators were adequate to handle the light passenger traffic of the metro in the early years, they could not cope with today's volume of passengers. Fortunately, the escalator was invented not long after the elevator came into production and is capable of shifting up to 10,000 people an hour along its moving treads.

Today's escalator is the result of two inventions. In 1882 Jesse Reno designed and patented a moving inclined ramp featuring cleated triangular platforms on a continuously operating belt. Like the steps on today's escalators, these platforms were combed to slot over one another as they flattened out at the top and bottom of the system. Unlike modern escalators, you had to hop off sideways when you reached the top. The purpose of combing the steps was to ensure that a soft shoe could not be drawn between the steps as they began to flatten out. Otherwise, as the lower step rose to meet the one above it, the friction of the shoe against it might cause the shoe to be drawn into the gap between the steps. In 1892 George Wheeler

independently patented a flat step "inclined elevator" with a handrail. His invention was developed by Charles D. Seeberger and the Otis Elevator Company into a flat step escalator that was exhibited at the Paris Exposition in 1900. By 1922 the Otis escalator combined Reno's cleated steps and combs with Seeberger's flat step, to become the forerunner of the modern escalator, where you step off in the direction of travel on reaching the top.

Escalators operate at a constant speed whether they are carrying a great number of people at rush hour or just their own weight. Historically, this speed was 27m (90ft) or 36m (120ft) per minute. Speeds have now been standardized at 30m (100ft) per minute, although faster speeds are in use on some very long escalators – for example in the deep stations of the Moscow, Kiev, and Leningrad metros – to reduce the journey time. In Kiev the rise is 65m (213ft), a record length for an inclined escalator, and speeds as high as 60m (200ft) per minute are used.

The normal angle of incline of an escalator is 30 degrees, but this can vary from 27.3 degrees (the incline of a public staircase) to 35 degrees.

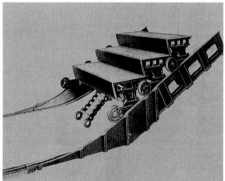

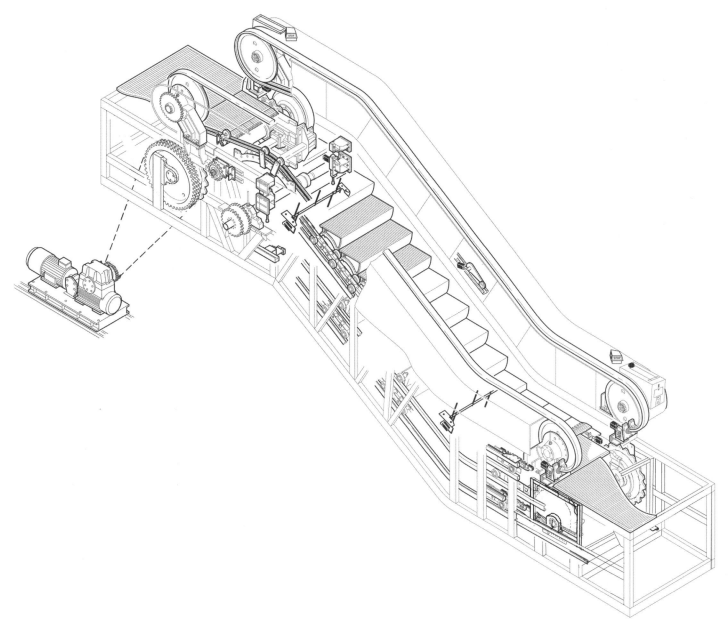

below **The cleverly illuminated escalator box and platform lighting of the new Heron Quays station on London's Docklands Light Rail, designed by Alsop Architects.**

right and far right **The "Tunnel of Light" in Nydalen Station on the Oslo metro surrounds the entry escalator shaft. It is based on 1,800 neon lights and 44 loudspeakers placed behind the enclosing glass surface. Each season has a distinctive mellow sound with a particular light pattern sequence, which is triggered by sensors on the escalator in response to passenger movement.**

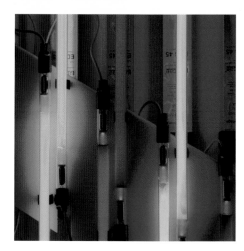

The 35-degree escalator will take up less volume but is limited to a 6m (20ft) rise and the standard operating speed for safety reasons.

The number of flat steps a passenger encounters stepping onto the escalator is extremely important. Observations have shown that the greater the number of flat steps before the treads begin to rise, the more easily passengers adjust to the moving escalator. Generally the greatest number of flat steps is deployed on high-speed and high-rise escalators.

In addition to the speed of travel, the width of the step is a key factor in determining the capacity of an escalator. The wider the step, the greater the number it can carry at the same operating speed. The smallest practical width of 60cm (24in) for a step will support only one person, while the widest 1m (40in) step allows a person with luggage or two adults to ride side by side on it. A further advantage of the 1m (40in) wide step is that if all the riders stand to one side, people in a hurry can pass them by on the other. Typically, a 60cm (24in) wide step operating at 30m (100ft) per minute and inclined at 30 degrees has a capacity of 5,626 persons per hour, while a 1m (40in) wide step has a capacity of 9,002 persons per hour.

The escalator drive wheel motors, the step chain, and conveyor belt are housed within a steel truss frame that spans between the floors. The steel truss is enclosed in metal panelling so that the guts of drive mechanism and moving parts of the escalator assembly are neatly hidden from view – one of the reasons that this remarkably efficient and durable piece of technology is so easy to take for granted.

maps

How do you get from here to there and then back again in quick time on the metro? Use the metro map, of course, where the stations and lines are so clearly set out, making it easy to check the name of the nearest station and the line to catch to get to your street.

It wasn't always as this easy, however. The diagrammatic illustration of the metro network with each line shown in a different colour and stations marked as circles or squares was first conceived in the 1930s and not fully developed until the 1940s. Up until then, the metro route maps were drawn as topographic maps, to scale, with thin lines superimposing the metro route over the streets, building names, and landmarks, as well as the background colours for rivers, waterways, and parkland spaces. It was information overload.

The early maps were printed in black and white or dull sepia tones. The free, brightly coloured maps that we take for granted today were not available because good colour printing with coloured inks and linen-quality paper was a luxury. Can you imagine trying to distinguish the myriad network routes of a modern metro system on a faded black and white print under a flickering, yellow light in 1910? Fortunately there were not that many lines to choose from and not very many stations to pick out in those days. But there would come a time in every city and on every metro network when a better more legible map would be essential.

Chicago was one of the first cities in the world to have an elevated light rail network built through the city centre. At one time it had the largest railway interchange in the USA. The decision was taken quite early on that underground travel was not a good idea and so it stuck with the elevated "metro". As the years rolled by and the city grew, and buildings started breaking through the clouds and the rest of America was dismantling its obsolete elevated lines for cleaner, faster, underground rail, the Chicago Transit Authority (CTA) persevered with its elevated metro. It was a looping network

left **The 1954 CTA (Chicago) network map** also features roads, landmarks, and topographic information. Combined with the limited colours, the result is a map that is hard to decipher.

below **The latest Chicago map is very easy to assimilate:** the loop area is enlarged and the graphics well defined with strong contrasting colours.

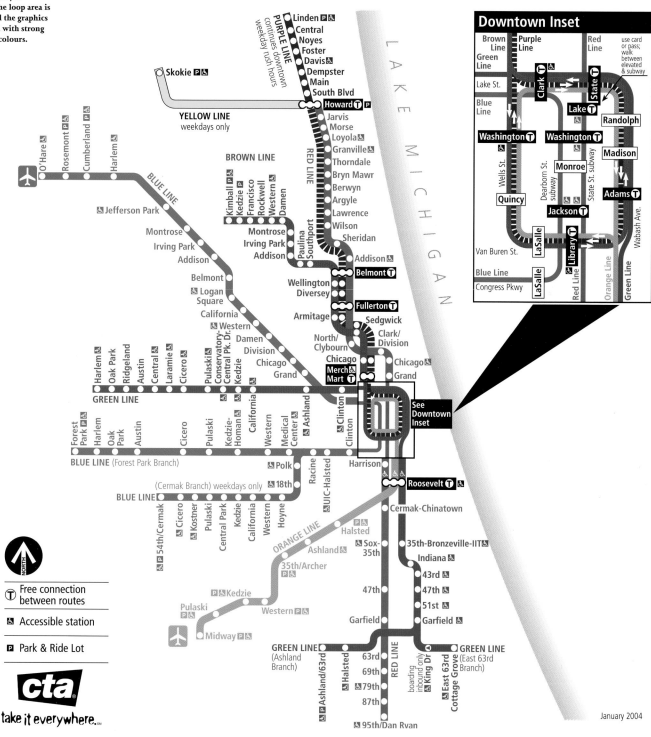

LAKE MICHIGAN

Downtown Inset

| Brown Line | Purple Line | | Red Line | use card or pass; walk between elevated & subway |
| Green Line | | | | |

Lake St.

Blue Line

Clark ⊤ | State ⊤

Lake ⊤

Randolph

Washington ⊤ | Washington ⊤

Madison

Monroe

Quincy

Jackson ⊤

Adams ⊤

Van Buren St.

LaSalle | Library ⊤

Blue Line

LaSalle

Congress Pkwy

Wells St.
Dearborn St. subway
State St. subway
Red Line
Orange Line
Green Line
Wabash Ave.

See Downtown Inset

PURPLE LINE continues downtown weekday rush hours

Linden P &
Central
Noyes
Foster
Davis &
Dempster
Main
South Blvd
Howard ⊤ P
Jarvis
Morse
Loyola &
Granville
Thorndale
Bryn Mawr
Berwyn
Argyle
Lawrence
Wilson
Sheridan
Addison &
Belmont ⊤
Wellington
Diversey
Fullerton ⊤
Sedgwick
Armitage
Clark/ Division
North/ Clybourn
Chicago
Grand

Skokie P &

YELLOW LINE weekdays only

RED LINE

BROWN LINE

Kimball P & Kedzie P
Francisco
Rockwell
Western &
Damen
Montrose
Irving Park
Addison
Paulina
Southport

Chicago &
Grand

O'Hare &
Rosemont P &
Cumberland P &
Harlem &

BLUE LINE

Jefferson Park &

Montrose
Irving Park
Addison
Belmont
Logan Square
California
Western &
Damen
Division
Chicago
Grand

Merch & Mart ⊤

Harlem &
Oak Park
Ridgeland
Austin
Central &
Laramie &
Cicero
Pulaski
Conservatory- Central Pk. Dr.
Kedzie
California
Western
Ashland
Clinton
Clinton

GREEN LINE

Forest Park P &
Harlem
Oak Park
Austin
Cicero
Pulaski
Kedzie- Homan
California
Western
Medical Center &
Ashland
Clinton
Clinton

BLUE LINE (Forest Park Branch)

Polk
Racine
UIC-Halsted
18th

(Cermak Branch) weekdays only

BLUE LINE

54th/Cermak
Cicero
Kostner
Pulaski
Central Park
Kedzie
California
Western
Hoyne

ORANGE LINE

Halsted
Ashland
35th/Archer
Kedzie
Pulaski
Western P &
Midway P &

Harrison
Roosevelt ⊤ &
Cermak-Chinatown
Sox- 35th
35th-Bronzeville-IIT &
Indiana &
43rd &
47th &
51st &
Garfield &

47th
Garfield

GREEN LINE (Ashland Branch)

Ashland/63rd
Halsted
63rd
69th
79th
87th
95th/Dan Rvan

RED LINE

King Dr
boarding inbound only

East 63rd
Cottage Grove

GREEN LINE (East 63rd Branch)

NORTH

⊤ Free connection between routes

& Accessible station

P Park & Ride Lot

cta
take it everywhere.℠

January 2004

below **On the Paris Métro map of 1939 the streets and other topographical details were removed for improved clarity, but as the layout was to scale, the map looked cramped and was not easy to read.**

right **The latest RATP map has greatly improved the legibility of the plan by using a diagrammatic layout, although the colours of the different lines are perhaps too diffuse for easy recognition.**

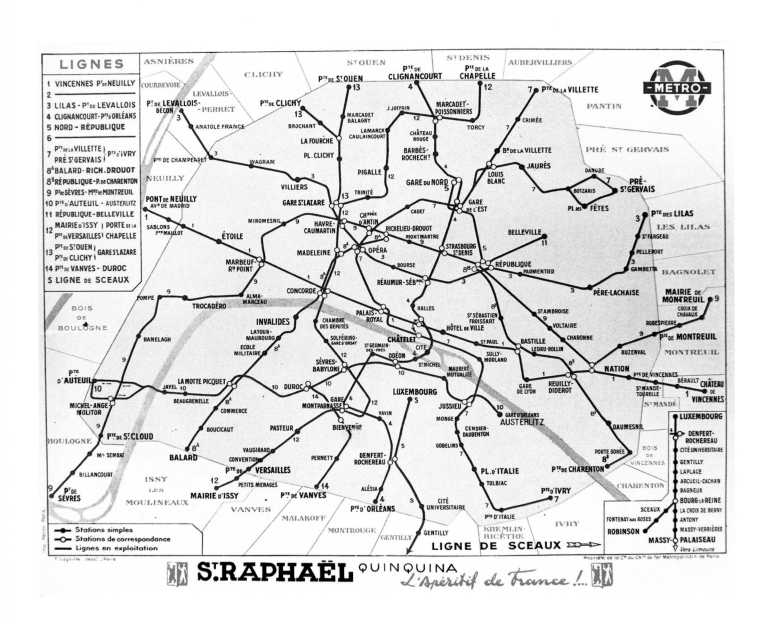

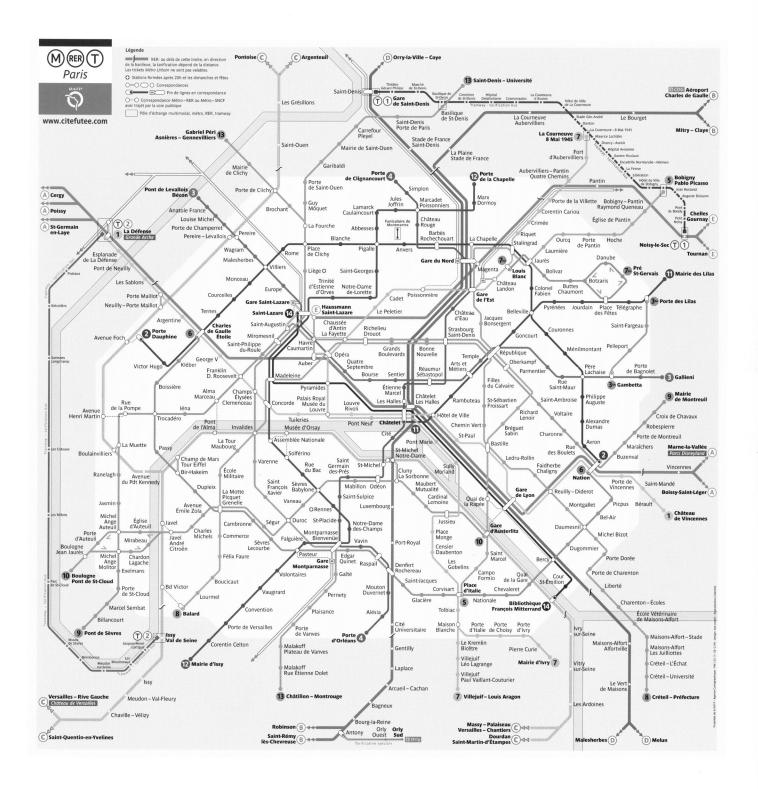

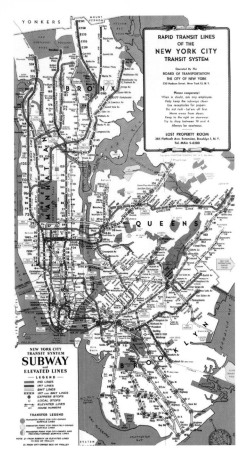

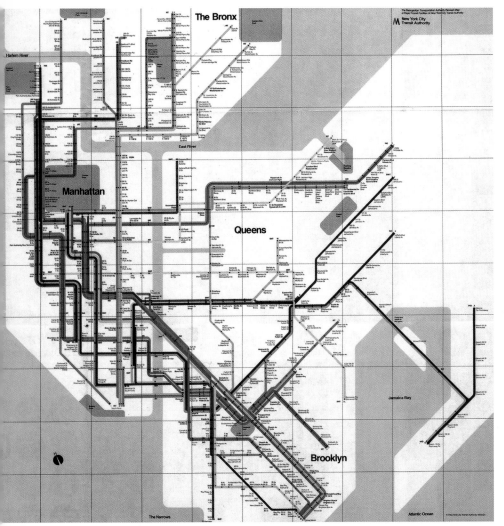

left The map of New York's subway in 1948 was well designed for a topographical map: the colour of network lines was easy to see, but the station names were bunched together and difficult to read.

below Massimo Vignelli's 1972 replacement was a work of art and was acknowledged as one of the finest diagrammatic layouts of a subway map. But it was instantly disliked by New Yorkers because it was too radical and stylized.

through downtown Chicago, supported on steelwork that straddled the streets with the trains running level with the third floors of buildings. The CTA network was simple and uncomplicated, but it was not until the 1970s that a brightly coloured fold-out diagram of the network was printed. For many years the elevated rail was printed over street maps with the loop highlighted in the centre of the paper.

The early Paris Métro maps offered much the same fare, with metro routes superimposed over street plans where they were shown as coloured lines running down the centre of the streets. (The underground generally followed the street plan, as much of the work was cut and cover construction down the middle of the road.) By 1939 there was improvement in map clarity, when the clutter of the street network and SNCF (surface rail) lines was removed and circle and bars were introduced to show the stations. But it took the RATP until the early 1970s to produce truly clear, easy-to-read diagrams of the Paris Métro.

The Mass Transit Authority of New York struggled to develop a simplified metro map even after the private metro companies were unified under the MTA in the 1940s. Until then, each network authority issued their own metro maps based on topographical street maps. Commuters would have to carry a handful of maps if their journey meant a change of network along the chosen route. A diagrammatic and well-drawn metro map was eventually produced in 1959, with all the network lines shown, and this remained the basis for the New York metro map for many years. It was replaced by a specially commissioned map by Massimo Vignelli in 1972, which was regarded as one of the finest examples of graphic design at the time. Utilizing 45-degree diagonals for the first time in the USA, with even spaces between stations, neat symbols, and bold colouring of lines, this was close to the example of the London Underground map. It was anticipated that the Vignelli map, when issued, would do for long-suffering New York commuters what Harry Beck's map had been providing for London commuters since 1933. Unfortunately, beautiful and orderly though it was, it was not well

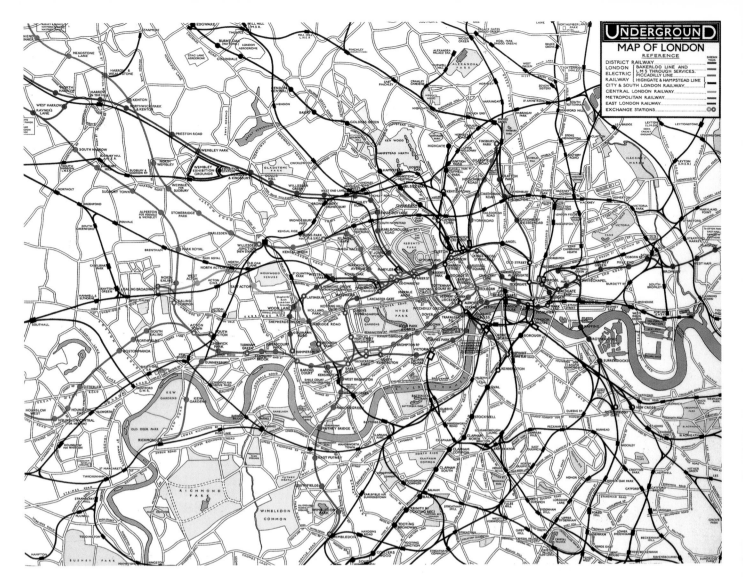

It was difficult for the cartographer to mark station names on the 1927 London Underground map (which was based on the street plan), especially in the congested central area.

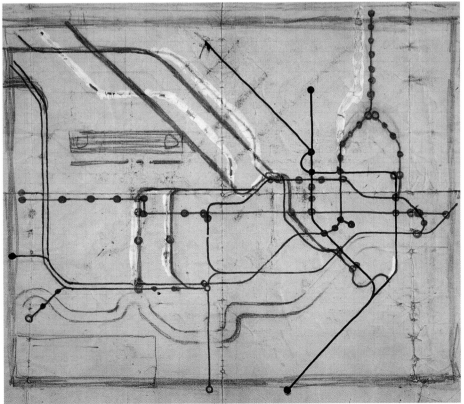

above It was difficult for the cartographer to mark station names on the 1927 London Underground map (which was based on the street plan), especially in the congested central area.

right Harry Beck's original sketch in an exercise book for his iconic diagram of the London Underground.

below The 1949 version of Beck's layout of the London Underground map was considered the best design he ever produced – and the finest subway map ever.

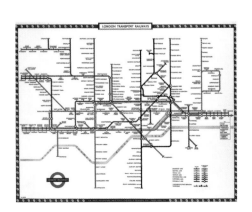

below **The Athens metro map has mountains, main streets, and green spaces included, but the graphics are so neat and orderly that these features do not detract from the legibility of station names or the clarity of network routes.**

right, top **The Osaka metro network is stylized to the point of being almost abstract, with no link to any physical landmarks of the city, nor the sea, which is close by.**

right, bottom **The current St Petersburg metro map is a very symmetrical diagram composed of strong lines running vertically on the page with station symbols laid out like ping–pong balls along the route. Land mass and rivers are softly outlined in the background.**

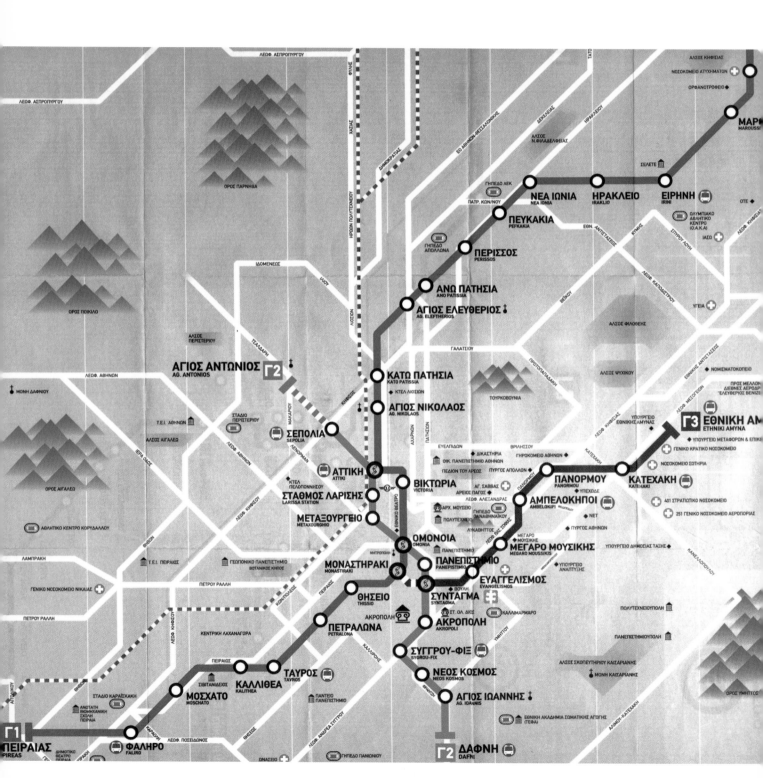

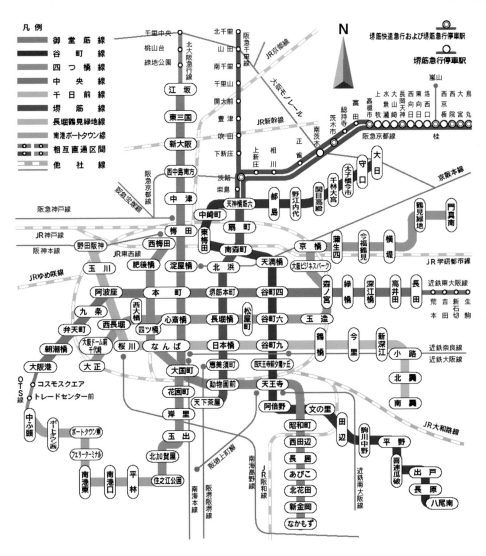

received by the travelling public, who thought it confusing, cryptic, and too radical. It did not last long and was replaced by a largely undistinguished but practical map based on a topographical scale with the lines idealized as curving, with bends and loops.

Henry C. Beck – Harry to his friends – was an engineering draughtsman who in 1931 made a sketch diagram of the London Underground network that was to change metro map design for ever. He tidied up the topographical layout of the original map by straightening the lines, using 45-degree diagonals instead of curves, and spacing the stations evenly. He selected the Central Line as his horizontal baseline and then drew in the rest of the network. He imagined that he was using a magnifying glass over the central map area to present these routes and stations on a larger scale. This was to give the many interchange stations in the central area space and clarity. From his initial sketch, made across two pages of an exercise book, he worked the map up to a presentation visual. He used blobs to denote stations and rings for interchange stations. Beck showed his idea to his colleagues, who encouraged him to submit it to the Publicity Department of London Underground. They rejected the idea, suggesting that it was too radical and revolutionary for people to accept. Beck did not give up and a year later resubmitted the map, knowing that the previous head of publicity had retired and there was a new man in the chair. This time they said yes, they would print it. In January 1933, some 750,000 copies of Beck's map were printed and a month later another 100,000. The map was popular with underground commuters: its revolutionary

design brought clarity and understanding to a complex map that had not been user friendly.

Over the years there have been improvements to Beck's design. The current map, made by Paul Garbutt in 1964, is based on Beck's design, capturing the essence of the original diagrammatic layout but adding a few neater touches, for example thickness of line, better station symbols and grouping of suburban routes across the page. Beck's design influenced map making worldwide. The few examples of modern metro maps shown here and in the gazetteer that follows give some idea of the sophistication of this art. There is reverse printing on black backgrounds, the strong use of colours, stylized overlays, strings of fine lines to map out complex networks, and carefully chosen lettering to make words legible in small print.

metro gazetteer

In any book like this there has to be a limit on the number of metro systems that can be described and reviewed. It is far better to illustrate generously stations selected for review than to restrict them to one or two images in order to double the entries. Which two images from Stockholm's 80 artistic stations do you pick? Which of the 40 stations on the Brussels metro would you exclude? We have avoided putting ourselves in such an impossible position. To make amends for ignoring many delightful metro stations, the list below gives some basic facts on the metro systems in existence today. If a network is under construction but has not yet opened it has not been included. This list was compiled from data found in **World Metro Systems** by Paul Garbutt (1996) and **Jane's Urban Transport Systems 2003/4**. Where there were large discrepancies between references we have made the best educated guess at the figure to use. All the systems are underground railways, which may have surface rail sections. The exceptions are noted in the operator and track gauge columns. A blank in a column means there has been no information available.

Key   rail – current rail
overhead – overhead high voltage wire
side beam – current rail above rail track to one side

ARGENTINA
buenos aires
operator	Metrovias
year open	1913
route length (km)	44.7
track gauge (m)	1.435
number of stations	63
power supply	1,500v/1100v/550v
current collection	overhead rail
wheel type	steel
passengers (mill/yr)	254

ARMENIA
yerevan
operator	Metro
year open	1981
route length (km)	13
track gauge (m)	1.520
number of stations	10
power supply	825v
current collection	rail
wheel type	steel
passengers (mill/yr)	36

AUSTRALIA
sydney
operator	CGEA light surface rail
year open	1997
route length (km)	12
track gauge (m)	1.435
number of stations	-
power supply	750v
current collection	-
wheel type	-
passengers (mill/yr)	-

AUSTRIA
vienna
operator	Wiener Stadtwerke
year open	1976
route length (km)	43.6
track gauge (m)	1.435
number of stations	62
power supply	750v
current collection	rail
wheel type	steel
passengers (mill/yr)	299.4

AZERBAIJAN
baku
operator	Metro
year open	1967
route length (km)	29
track gauge (m)	1.524
number of stations	18
power supply	825v
current collection	rail
wheel type	steel
passengers (mill/yr)	160

BELARUS
minsk
operator	Metro
year open	1984
route length (km)	18.5
track gauge (m)	1.524
number of stations	18
power supply	825v
current collection	rail
wheel type	steel
passengers (mill/yr)	139

BELGIUM
brussels
operator	STIB
year open	1976
route length (km)	40.5
track gauge (m)	1.435
number of stations	52
power supply	900v
current collection	rail
wheel type	steel
passengers (mill/yr)	85.9

BRAZIL
belo horizonte
operator	CBTU
year open	1986
route length (km)	21.3
track gauge (m)	1.600
number of stations	13
power supply	3,000v
current collection	overhead
wheel type	steel
passengers (mill/yr)	19.2

porto alegre
operator	Trensurb
year open	1985
route length (km)	31.5
track gauge (m)	1.600
number of stations	16
power supply	3,000v
current collection	overhead
wheel type	steel
passengers (mill/yr)	38.6

recife
operator	Metrorec
year open	1985
route length (km)	52.5
track gauge (m)	1.600
number of stations	27
power supply	3,000v

current collection	overhead
wheel type	steel
passengers (mill/yr)	40.7

rio de janeiro
operator	Metro
year open	1979
route length (km)	34.9
track gauge (m)	1.600
number of stations	32
power supply	750v
current collection	rail
wheel type	steel
passengers (mill/yr)	95

são paulo
operator	Metro
year open	1974
route length (km)	49.2
track gauge (m)	1.600
number of stations	46
power supply	750v
current collection	rail
wheel type	steel
passengers (mill/yr)	690

CANADA
montreal
operator	STCUM
year open	1966
route length (km)	65
track gauge (m)	-
number of stations	65
power supply	750v
current collection	side beams
wheel type	rubber
passengers (mill/yr)	197

toronto
operator	TTC
year open	1954
route length (km)	68.3
track gauge (m)	1.495
number of stations	59
power supply	600v
current collection	rail
wheel type	steel
passengers (mill/yr)	158.7

vancouver
operator	Skytrain
year open	1986
route length (km)	28.8
track gauge (m)	1.435
number of stations	20
power supply	600v
current collection	rail
wheel type	steel
passengers (mill/yr)	24.1

above **Jinonice station on Line B of Prague metro, opened in 1988.**

below **A train heads downtown on Toronto's Yonge–University–Spadina Subway Line.**

CHILE
santiago de chile
operator	Metro de Santiago
year open	1975
route length (km)	37.6
track gauge (m)	1.435
number of stations	47
power supply	750v
current collection	side beams
wheel type	rubber
passengers (mill/yr)	200

CHINA
beijing
operator	BMTRC
year open	1969
route length (km)	42
track gauge (m)	1.435
number of stations	29
power supply	750v
current collection	rail
wheel type	steel
passengers (mill/yr)	530

guangzhou
operator	Subway
year open	1998
route length (km)	18.5
track gauge (m)	1.435
number of stations	16
power supply	-
current collection	rail
wheel type	steel
passengers (mill/yr)	-

hong kong
operator	MTR

above **Bao-Shaw Road station on the Shanghai metro, one of the newest in the world.**

bottom **Neil Dawsons art work "Birds of a Feather" floats above Tsing Yi station on Hong Kong's MTR.**

year open	1979
route length (km)	84
track gauge (m)	1.435
number of stations	44
power supply	1,500v
current collection	overhead
wheel type	steel
passengers (mill/yr)	804

shanghai

operator	Metro
year open	1993
route length (km)	16.1
track gauge (m)	1.435
number of stations	13
power supply	1,500v
current collection	overhead
wheel type	steel
passengers (mill/yr)	87

tianjin

operator	Metro
year open	1980
route length (km)	7.8
track gauge (m)	1.435
number of stations	8
power supply	750v
current collection	rail
wheel type	steel
passengers (mill/yr)	10.5

COLOMBIA
medellín

operator	ETMVA
year open	1995
route length (km)	28.8
track gauge (m)	1.435
number of stations	25
power supply	1,500v
current collection	overhead
wheel type	steel
passengers (mill/yr)	62

CZECH REPUBLIC
prague

operator	DP Metro
year open	1974
route length (km)	50.1
track gauge (m)	1.435
number of stations	51

power supply	750v
current collection	rail
wheel type	steel
passengers (mill/yr)	442

EGYPT
cairo
operator	NAT
year open	1987
route length (km)	42.5
track gauge (m)	1.435
number of stations	33
power supply	1,500v
current collection	overhead
wheel type	steel
passengers (mill/yr)	300

FINLAND
helsinki
operator	Metro
year open	1982
route length (km)	21.3
track gauge (m)	1.524
number of stations	16
power supply	750v
current collection	rail
wheel type	steel
passengers (mill/yr)	52.8

FRANCE
lille
operator	Metro (VAL)
year open	1983
route length (km)	45
track gauge (m)	1.435
number of stations	60
power supply	750v
current collection	side beams
wheel type	rubber
passengers (mill/yr)	54.1

lyons
operator	SLTC Metro
year open	1978
route length (km)	27.5
track gauge (m)	1.435
number of stations	39
power supply	750v
current collection	side beams
wheel type	rubber
passengers (mill/yr)	125

marseille
operator	RTM
year open	1978
route length (km)	19.5
track gauge (m)	2.000
number of stations	24
power supply	750v
current collection	side beams
wheel type	rubber
passengers (mill/yr)	56

paris
operator	RATP
year open	1900
route length (km)	201.4
track gauge (m)	1.435
number of stations	372
power supply	750v
current collection	rail/side beams
wheel type	rubber
passengers (mill/yr)	1,170

toulouse
operator	Semvat (MTD)
year open	1993
route length (km)	10
track gauge (m)	-
number of stations	15
power supply	750v
current collection	side beams
wheel type	rubber
passengers (mill/yr)	30.5

GEORGIA
tblisi
operator	Metro
year open	1965
route length (km)	23
track gauge (m)	1.524
number of stations	20
power supply	825v
current collection	rail
wheel type	steel
passengers (mill/yr)	144

GERMANY
berlin
operator	BVG
year open	1902
route length (km)	164.7
track gauge (m)	1.435
number of stations	167
power supply	780v
current collection	rail
wheel type	steel
passengers (mill/yr)	450

frankfurt
operator	Stadtbahn
year open	1968
route length (km)	56.2
track gauge (m)	1.435
number of stations	82
power supply	600v
current collection	overhead
wheel type	steel
passengers (mill/yr)	92.6

hamburg
operator	HHA

above **Cairo metro, the only metro system on the African continent so far.**

below **The Paris Métro was the first to use rubber-wheeled trains. Today, Montreal, Mexico, Santiago de Chile, and Sapporo also use this system.**

year open	1912
route length (km)	101
track gauge (m)	1.435
number of stations	89
power supply	750v
current collection	rail
wheel type	steel
passengers (mill/yr)	176

munich

operator	SWM Metro
year open	1971
route length (km)	85
track gauge (m)	1.435
number of stations	89
power supply	750v
current collection	rail
wheel type	steel
passengers (mill/yr)	293

nuremberg

operator	VAG Metro
year open	1972
route length (km)	30
track gauge (m)	1.435
number of stations	39
power supply	750v
current collection	rail
wheel type	steel
passengers (mill/yr)	81.7

wuppertal

operator	WSW
year open	1901
route length (km)	13.3
track gauge (m)	suspended monorail
number of stations	20
power supply	600v
current collection	rail
wheel type	steel
passengers (mill/yr)	25

GREECE
athens

operator	ISAP
year open	1991
route length (km)	25.8 (estimated)
track gauge (m)	1.435
number of stations	23
power supply	750v/600v
current collection	rail overhead

wheel type	steel
passengers (mill/yr)	85 (estimated)

HUNGARY
budapest

operator	BKV
year open	1896
route length (km)	31.7
track gauge (m)	1.435
number of stations	78
power supply	825v
current collection	rail
wheel type	steel
passengers (mill/yr)	323

INDIA
calcutta

operator	Metro
year open	1984
route length (km)	16.6
track gauge (m)	1.676
number of stations	17
power supply	750v
current collection	rail
wheel type	steel
passengers (mill/yr)	30

delhi

operator	DMRC
year open	2003
route length (km)	11
track gauge (m)	1.676
number of stations	-
power supply	-
current collection	-
wheel type	-
passengers (mill/yr)	-

madras

operator	Metro surface light rail
year open	1991
route length (km)	5.0
track gauge (m)	1.676
number of stations	5
power supply	750v
current collection	rail
wheel type	steel
passengers (mill/yr)	-

ITALY
genoa

operator	AMT
year open	1990
route length (km)	3.4
track gauge (m)	1.435
number of stations	3
power supply	750v
current collection	overhead
wheel type	steel
passengers (mill/yr)	3.5

milan

operator	ATM metro
year open	1964
route length (km)	69.3
track gauge (m)	1.435
number of stations	84
power supply	750v/1,500v
current collection	rail overhead
wheel type	steel
passengers (mill/yr)	344

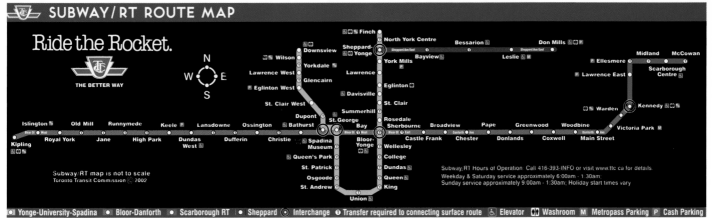

Ride the Rocket.

THE BETTER WAY

N W E S

Finch · North York Centre · Bessarion · Don Mills · Midland · McCowan

Downsview · Sheppard-Yonge · Sheppard Ave East · Bayview · Leslie · Ellesmere · Scarborough Centre

Wilson · York Mills

Yorkdale · Lawrence · Lawrence East

Lawrence West · Eglinton · Warden · Kennedy

Glencairn · Davisville

Eglinton West · St. Clair · Victoria Park

St. Clair West · Summerhill

Dupont · Rosedale · Sherbourne · Broadview · Pape · Greenwood · Woodbine

St. George · Bay · Castle Frank · Chester · Donlands · Coxwell · Main Street

Islington · Old Mill · Runnymede · Keele · Lansdowne · Ossington · Bathurst · Bloor-Yonge

Kipling · Royal York · Jane · High Park · Dundas West · Dufferin · Christie · Spadina · Wellesley

Spadina Museum · College

Queen's Park · Dundas

St. Patrick · Queen

Osgoode · King

St. Andrew · Union

Subway/RT map is not to scale
Toronto Transit Commission © 2002

Subway/RT Hours of Operation Call 416-393-INFO or visit www.ttc.ca for details.
Weekday & Saturday service approximately 6:00am - 1:30am;
Sunday service approximately 9:00am - 1:30am; Holiday start times vary

Yonge-University-Spadina · Bloor-Danforth · Scarborough RT · Sheppard · Interchange · Transfer required to connecting surface route · Elevator · Washroom · M Metropass Parking · P Cash Parking

above **The black background of the map for Toronto's metro makes a striking contrast with the norm.**

naples

operator	Metronapoli
year open	1993
route length (km)	9.5
track gauge (m)	1.435
number of stations	9
power supply	1500v
current collection	overhead
wheel type	steel
passengers (mill/yr)	39.5

rome

operator	COTRAL
year open	1955
route length (km)	33.5
track gauge (m)	1.435
number of stations	43
power supply	1,500v
current collection	overhead
wheel type	steel
passengers (mill/yr)	245

JAPAN

chiba

operator	Chiba Monorail
year open	1988
route length (km)	14
track gauge (m)	suspended
number of stations	18
power supply	1,500v
current collection	rail
wheel type	-
passengers (mill/yr)	15

fukuoka

operator	FMTB
year open	1981
route length (km)	17.8
track gauge (m)	1.067
number of stations	20
power supply	1,500v
current collection	overhead
wheel type	steel
passengers (mill/yr)	108

kitakyushu

operator	KKT
year open	1985
route length (km)	8.4
track gauge (m)	monorail
number of stations	12
power supply	1,500v
current collection	beam
wheel type	-
passengers (mill/yr)	11.9

kobe

operator	KMTB
year open	1977
route length (km)	22.7
track gauge (m)	1.435
number of stations	16
power supply	1,500v
current collection	overhead
wheel type	steel
passengers (mill/yr)	95

operator	KNTC
year open	1981
route length (km)	10.9
track gauge (m)	-
number of stations	15
power supply	600v
current collection	side rail
wheel type	rubber
passengers (mill/yr)	29.5

kyoto

operator	KMTB
year open	1981
route length (km)	26.4
track gauge (m)	1.435
number of stations	28
power supply	1,500v
current collection	overhead
wheel type	steel
passengers (mill/yr)	111

nagoya

operator	NMTB
year open	1957
route length (km)	78
track gauge (m)	1.435/1.067
number of stations	87
power supply	600v/1500v
current collection	rail/overhead
wheel type	steel
passengers (mill/yr)	408

osaka

operator	OMTB
year open	1933
route length (km)	105.8
track gauge (m)	1.435
number of stations	99
power supply	750v/1,500v
current collection	rail/overhead
wheel type	steel
passengers (mill/yr)	855

operator	ICTS
year open	1981

wheel type	steel
passengers (mill/yr)	2,041
operator	TBTMG
year open	1960
route length (km)	109
track gauge (m)	1.435/1.372/1.067
number of stations	105
power supply	1,500v
current collection	overhead
wheel type	steel
passengers (mill/yr)	600

yokohama

operator	YMTB
year open	1972
route length (km)	40.4
track gauge (m)	1.435
number of stations	27
power supply	750v
current collection	rail
wheel type	steel
passengers (mill/yr)	150
operator	New Transit
year open	1989
route length (km)	-
track gauge (m)	-
number of stations	14
power supply	750v
current collection	rail
wheel type	rubber
passengers (mill/yr)	-

MALAYSIA
kuala lumpur

operator	STAR elevated light rail
year open	1996
route length (km)	27
track gauge (m)	1.435
number of stations	21
power supply	750v
current collection	rail
wheel type	steel
passengers (mill/yr)	36

MEXICO
mexico

operator	STC Metro
year open	1969
route length (km)	201
track gauge (m)	1.435
number of stations	175
power supply	750v
current collection	side beam

route length (km)	6.6
track gauge (m)	-
number of stations	8
power supply	600v
current collection	side beams
wheel type	rubber
passengers (mill/yr)	22.5
operator	OKT
year open	1990
route length (km)	6.7
track gauge (m)	monorail
number of stations	5
power supply	1500v
current collection	beam
wheel type	-
passengers (mill/yr)	1.4

sapporo

operator	SCTB
year open	1971
route length (km)	48
track gauge (m)	-
number of stations	49
power supply	750v/1,500v
current collection	rail/overhead
wheel type	rubber
passengers (mill/yr)	206

sendai

operator	SCTB
year open	1987
route length (km)	14.8
track gauge (m)	1.067
number of stations	17
power supply	1,500v
current collection	overhead
wheel type	steel
passengers (mill/yr)	60.1

tokyo

operator	TRTA
year open	1927
route length (km)	177
track gauge (m)	1.435/1.067
number of stations	164
power supply	600v/1,500v
current collection	rail/overhead

| wheel type | rubber |
| passengers (mill/yr) | 1,434 |

monterrey

operator	Metrorey light rail
year open	1991
route length (km)	23.5
track gauge (m)	1.435
number of stations	24
power supply	1,500v
current collection	overhead
wheel type	steel
passengers (mill/yr)	36.2

NETHERLANDS
amsterdam

operator	GVB elevated
year open	1977
route length (km)	51
track gauge (m)	1.435
number of stations	49
power supply	750v/600v
current collection	rail/overhead
wheel type	steel
passengers (mill/yr)	49 (estimated)

rotterdam

operator	RET/Sneltram
year open	1968
route length (km)	76
track gauge (m)	1.435
number of stations	42
power supply	750v
current collection	rail/overhead
wheel type	steel
passengers (mill/yr)	84

NORTH KOREA
pyongyang

operator	Metro
year open	1973
route length (km)	22.5
track gauge (m)	1.435
number of stations	17
power supply	825v
current collection	rail
wheel type	steel
passengers (mill/yr)	42

NORWAY
oslo

operator	Sporveier
year open	1966
route length (km)	80
track gauge (m)	1.435
number of stations	101
power supply	750v
current collection	rail
wheel type	steel
passengers (mill/yr)	59

PERU
lima

operator	AATE
year open	1995
route length (km)	20.8
track gauge (m)	1.435
number of stations	–
power supply	1,500v
current collection	rail
wheel type	steel
passengers (mill/yr)	–

PHILIPPINES
manila

operator	LRTA Metro elevated rail
year open	1984
route length (km)	32
track gauge (m)	1.435
number of stations	30
power supply	750v
current collection	overhead
wheel type	steel
passengers (mill/yr)	134

POLAND
warsaw

operator	Metro
year open	1995
route length (km)	11.2
track gauge (m)	1.435
number of stations	11
power supply	750v
current collection	rail
wheel type	steel
passengers (mill/yr)	48.8

PORTUGAL
lisbon

operator	ML
year open	1959
route length (km)	19
track gauge (m)	1.435
number of stations	25
power supply	750v
current collection	rail
wheel type	steel
passengers (mill/yr)	139

ROMANIA
bucharest

operator	Metrorex RA
year open	1979
route length (km)	63
track gauge (m)	1.435
number of stations	45
power supply	750v
current collection	rail
wheel type	steel
passengers (mill/yr)	110

below An Oslo metro train. Oslo metro, known as the T-Bane (from *Tunnelbane*), was opened in 1966.

СХЕМА ЛИНИЙ МОСКОВСКОГО МЕТРОПОЛИТЕНА
ИМЕНИ В.И.ЛЕНИНА

above **The 1970 Moscow Metro map. The Moscow network is almost entirely below ground, and has some extremely deep stations. Some were intended to double up as nuclear shelters.**

RUSSIAN FEDERATION
kiev
operator	Metro
year open	1960
route length (km)	43.2
track gauge (m)	1.524
number of stations	36
power supply	825v
current collection	rail
wheel type	steel
passengers (mill/yr)	365

moscow
operator	Metro
year open	1935
route length (km)	262
track gauge (m)	1.524
number of stations	160
power supply	825v
current collection	rail
wheel type	steel
passengers (mill/yr)	3,208

nizhniy novgorod
operator	Metro
year open	1985
route length (km)	13
track gauge (m)	1.524
number of stations	12
power supply	825v
current collection	rail
wheel type	steel
passengers (mill/yr)	66

novosibirsk
operator	Metro
year open	1985
route length (km)	13
track gauge (m)	1.524
number of stations	10
power supply	825v
current collection	rail

wheel type	steel
passengers (mill/yr)	82

st petersburg
operator	Metro
year open	1955
route length (km)	93
track gauge (m)	1.524
number of stations	56
power supply	825v
current collection	rail
wheel type	steel
passengers (mill/yr)	721

samara
operator	Metro
year open	1987
route length (km)	12.5
track gauge (m)	1.524
number of stations	14
power supply	825v
current collection	rail
wheel type	steel
passengers (mill/yr)	33

yekaterinburg
operator	Metro
year open	1992
route length (km)	12
track gauge (m)	1.524
number of stations	6
power supply	825v
current collection	rail
wheel type	steel
passengers (mill/yr)	-

SINGAPORE
operator	SMRT
year open	1987
route length (km)	83
track gauge (m)	1.435
number of stations	51
power supply	750v
current collection	overhead
wheel type	steel
passengers (mill/yr)	390

SOUTH KOREA
pusan
operator	PUTA
year open	1985
route length (km)	73
track gauge (m)	1.435
number of stations	73
power supply	1,500v
current collection	overhead
wheel type	steel
passengers (mill/yr)	224

seoul
operator	Subway
year open	1974
route length (km)	144
track gauge (m)	1.435
number of stations	114
power supply	1,500v
current collection	overhead
wheel type	steel
passengers (mill/yr)	1,388

SPAIN
barcelona
operator	TMB

year open	1924
route length (km)	81
track gauge (m)	1.674/1.435
number of stations	112
power supply	1,500v/1,200v
current collection	overhead/rail
wheel type	steel
passengers (mill/yr)	280

bilbao

operator	Metro
year open	1995
route length (km)	26.5
track gauge (m)	1.000
number of stations	23
power supply	1,500v
current collection	overhead
wheel type	steel
passengers (mill/yr)	41.5

madrid

operator	Metro
year open	1919
route length (km)	118.5
track gauge (m)	1.445
number of stations	163
power supply	600v
current collection	overhead
wheel type	steel
passengers (mill/yr)	413

SWEDEN
stockholm

operator	Metro
year open	1950
route length (km)	110
track gauge (m)	1.435
number of stations	100
power supply	650–750v
current collection	rail
wheel type	steel
passengers (mill/yr)	263

TAIWAN
taipei

operator	TRTC
year open	1996
route length (km)	10.9
track gauge (m)	-
number of stations	12
power supply	750v
current collection	side rail
wheel type	rubber
passengers (mill/yr)	35

THAILAND
bangkok

operator	BTS
year open	1999
route length (km)	16.8
track gauge (m)	1.435

number of stations	17
power supply	750v
current collection	rail
wheel type	steel
passengers (mill/yr)	270

TURKEY
ankara

operator	EGO
year open	1996
route length (km)	8.5
track gauge (m)	1.435
number of stations	11
power supply	750v
current collection	rail
wheel type	steel
passengers (mill/yr)	44

istanbul

operator	IUAS
year open	1989
route length (km)	19
track gauge (m)	1.435
number of stations	18
power supply	750v
current collection	overhead
wheel type	steel
passengers (mill/yr)	36

UNITED KINGDOM
glasgow

operator	SPTE
year open	1896
route length (km)	14.6
track gauge (m)	1.220
number of stations	15
power supply	600v
current collection	rail
wheel type	steel
passengers (mill/yr)	14.7

london

operator	LUL
year open	1863
route length (km)	392
track gauge (m)	1.435
number of stations	267
power supply	600v
current collection	rail
wheel type	steel
passengers (mill/yr)	832

operator	DLR (elevated)
year open	1987
route length (km)	26
track gauge (m)	1.435
number of stations	34
power supply	750v
current collection	rail
wheel type	steel
passengers (mill/yr)	28.6

newcastle

operator	Tyne and Wear PTE
year open	1980
route length (km)	59.1
track gauge (m)	1.435
number of stations	46
power supply	1500v
current collection	overhead
wheel type	steel
passengers (mill/yr)	39.5

left **A Line 3 station on Barcelona's metro system. Although Line 3 is one of the older lines, it was refurbished in the 1980s and has very modern rolling stock.**

below **A light display entertains the waiting passengers at Heron Quays station on London's DLR.**

above **The number 4 train travels through the Bronx on the New York metro.**

USA

atlanta

operator	MARTA
year open	1979
route length (km)	74
track gauge (m)	1.435
number of stations	36
power supply	750v
current collection	rail
wheel type	steel
passengers (mill/yr)	69.9

baltimore

operator	MMTA
year open	1983
route length (km)	24.9
track gauge (m)	1.435
number of stations	12
power supply	700v
current collection	rail
wheel type	steel
passengers (mill/yr)	12.8

boston

operator	MBTA
year open	1901
route length (km)	125
track gauge (m)	1.435
number of stations	84
power supply	600v
current collection	rail/overhead
wheel type	steel
passengers (mill/yr)	150

chicago

operator	CTA(elevated)
year open	1892
route length (km)	173
track gauge (m)	1.435
number of stations	140
power supply	600v
current collection	rail
wheel type	steel
passengers (mill/yr)	144

cleveland

operator	GCRTA
year open	1955
route length (km)	30.7
track gauge (m)	1.435
number of stations	18
power supply	600v
current collection	overhead
wheel type	steel
passengers (mill/yr)	5.6

detroit

operator	DTC
year open	1987
route length (km)	4.8
track gauge (m)	1.435
number of stations	13
power supply	600v
current collection	rail
wheel type	steel
passengers (mill/yr)	2.5

jacksonville

operator	JTA
year open	1989
route length (km)	4
track gauge (m)	-
number of stations	8

power supply	750v
current collection	side rail
wheel type	rubber
passengers (mill/yr)	0.8

los angeles

operator	LACMTA
year open	1993
route length (km)	28
track gauge (m)	1.435
number of stations	16
power supply	750v
current collection	rail
wheel type	steel
passengers (mill/yr)	12

miami

operator	Metro
year open	1984
route length (km)	33
track gauge (m)	1.435
number of stations	21
power supply	700v
current collection	rail
wheel type	steel
passengers (mill/yr)	14.5

new york

operator	NYCTA
year open	1904
route length (km)	398
track gauge (m)	1.435
number of stations	469
power supply	625v
current collection	rail
wheel type	steel
passengers (mill/yr)	1,132

operator	PATH
year open	1908
route length (km)	22.2
track gauge (m)	1.435
number of stations	13
power supply	650v
current collection	rail
wheel type	steel
passengers (mill/yr)	67

operator	Staten Island RT
year open	-
route length (km)	23
track gauge (m)	1.435
number of stations	22
power supply	600v
current collection	rail
wheel type	steel
passengers (mill/yr)	5.1

philadelphia

operator	SEPTA
year open	1908
route length (km)	41
track gauge (m)	1.581/
number of stations	62
power supply	625v
current collection	rail
wheel type	steel
passengers (mill/yr)	53.7

operator	PATCO
year open	1969
route length (km)	23.3
track gauge (m)	1.435

number of stations	13
power supply	685v
current collection	rail
wheel type	steel
passengers (mill/yr)	11.2

san francisco

operator	BART
year open	1972
route length (km)	153
track gauge (m)	1.676
number of stations	39
power supply	1000v
current collection	rail
wheel type	steel
passengers (mill/yr)	90

washington

operator	WMATA
year open	1976
route length (km)	166
track gauge (m)	1.435
number of stations	83
power supply	750v
current collection	rail
wheel type	steel
passengers (mill/yr)	153.6

UKRAINE
kharkov

operator	Metro
year open	1984
route length (km)	26
track gauge (m)	1.524
number of stations	27
power supply	750v
current collection	rail
wheel type	steel
passengers (mill/yr)	250

UZBEKISTAN
tashkent

operator	Metro
year open	1977
route length (km)	30
track gauge (m)	1.524
number of stations	26
power supply	825v
current collection	rail
wheel type	steel
passengers (mill/yr)	180

VENEZUELA
caracas

operator	Metro
year open	1983
route length (km)	41
track gauge (m)	1.435
number of stations	35
power supply	750v
current collection	rail
wheel type	steel
passengers (mill/yr)	325

below **Daniel Martinez's sculpture "For Your Intellectual Entertainment" at El Segundo Nash station on Los Angeles' Green Line. Architect: Escudero–Fribourg.**

bibliography

Annual Report 2002, BKV Publications

Art Dans Le Métro, STIB Service
Communication Impression, May 2000

Bousset, Dr Ing E.h. J. *Die Berliner U-Bahn*,
Verlag Von Wilhem Ernst & Sohn, 1935

Les Cahiers de la Memoire, Nos 1, 2, 8, and 9,
RATP Publications Series

Castleman, Craig. *Getting Up*, The MIT Press, 1982

Emmerson, Andrew. *The Underground Pioneers*, Capital
Transport Publishing, 2000

Garbutt, Paul. *World Metro Systems*, Capital Transport
Publishing, 2nd edn, 1997

Garland, Ken. *Mr Beck's Underground Map*, Capital Transport
Publishing, 1994

Greathead, J.H. "The City and South London Railway"
in Minutes of Proceedings of the Institution of Civil Engineers,
vol. CXXIII, 1896

Green, Oliver. *Underground Art*, Laurence King, 1990

Hacklesberger, Christoph. *U-Bahn: Subway Architecture In
Munich*, Prestel Verlag, 1997

Hardie, C.W. *Escalators and Passenger Conveyors*, London
Transport, 1975

Hardy, Brian. *The Berlin U-Bahn*, Capital Transport
Publishing, 1996

Hardy, Brian. *Paris Métro Handbook*, Capital Transport
Publishing, 3rd edn, 1999

Havers, H.C.P. *Underground Railways of the World*, Temple
Press Books, 1966

Hillman, Ellis and Richard Trench. *London Under London*,
John Murray, 1993

Hood, Clifton. *722 Miles*, The Johns Hopkins University
Press, 1993

Jane's Urban Transport Systems: 22nd Edition, 2003–2004, Jane's
Information Group

Kaganovicha, L.M. *Architecture of the Moscow Metro*,
Akademya Architektur, 1939

Knutton, Mike. *A Metro for Istanbul*, Alstom Transport
SA, 2002

Lawrence, David. *Underground Architecture*, Capital
Transport Publishing, 1994

Mathewson, Andrew and Derek Laval. *Brunel's Tunnel and
Where It Led*, Brunel Exhibition, London, 1992

McClean, Ian and John Wright. *Circles Under The Clyde*.
Capital Transport Publishing, 1997

Metro at 25, Washington Metropolitan Area Transit
Authority, 2001

The Millennium Underground, BKV Publications

"Naissance D'un Metro: Sur La Nouvelle Ligne 14", *La
vie du Rail & des Transports*, October 1998

Ovenden, Mark. *Metro Maps Of the World*, Capital Transport
Publishing, 2003

Sheppard Subway Public Art Program 2002, Toronto Transit
Commission pamphlet

Soderstrom, Goran. *Art Goes Underground: Art In the Stockholm
Metro*, Lettura, 1988

Strakosch, George R. (ed). *The Vertical Transportation
Handbook*, 3rd edn, John Wiley & Sons, 1998

Subways In Japan, Japan Subway Association, March 2002

Szechy, Karoly. *The Art Of Tunnelling*, Akademiai
Kiado, 1973

Taylor, Sheila. *The Moving Metropolis*, Laurence King, 2001

Third Annual Report of The West End Street Railway Company,
Boston, 1890

25 years of the Budapest Metro, BKV Publications

Vaughan, Adrian. *Isambard Kingdom Brunel*, John
Murray, 1991

index

picture credits

Mitchell Beazley would like to acknowledge and thank the following photographers and organizations who have provided images for use in this book.

Every attempt has been made to establish copyright ownership in pictures. We apologise should any omissions have been made, and upon notification will be pleased to make appropriate corrections in any future editions.

Key: a above, b below, c centre, l left, r right. ICE: Institution of Civil Engineers

Cover, front and back: Mark Thomas Photography

2-3 Transports Metropolitans de Barcelona; 6 RATP; 7 London's Transport Museum; 8 Chicago Transit Authority; 9 photo E Dixon; 11a RATP; 11b, 12 ALSTOM; 14a London's Transport Museum; 14b-15b, 15 ICE; 16a & b London's Transport Museum; 17a & b ICE; 18 London's Transport Museum; 19-20b ICE; 20a London's Transport Museum; 22a & b ICE; 23 London's Transport Museum; 24a ICE; 24b Sir Robert McAlpine Ltd, photo E Dixon; 25 WMATA, photo Paul Myatt; 26l & r Atlas Copco; 27 Toronto Transit Commission; 28a ICE; 28b RATP, photo Bruno Marguerite; 29 ALSTOM; 30 Brian Hardy; 31a London's Transport Museum; 31b Singapore MTR; 32-35 London's Transport Museum; 36-38 ICE; 39 Strathclyde Passenger Transport; 40a ICE; 40b-42 Budapest Metro; 43a & b Tourism Office of Budapest; 44-6 Courtesy of the State Transportation Library of Massachusetts; 47a & b ICE; 48-50 RATP; 51a ICE; 51b RATP, photo Bertrand Chabrol; 52-55a ICE; 55b BVG; 56a Topham/The Image Works/photo Monica Graff; 56b-61 ICE; 62 Mark Thomas Photography; 64-66a ICE; 66b, 67a Brian Hardy; 67b Capital Transport; 68 ICE; 69 Novosti Photo Library; 70l, a & br ICE; 71 Novosti Photo Library; 72-73 Mark Thomas Photography; 74 London's Transport Museum; 75a Christopher Woods; 75br & bl London's Transport Museum; 76 Christopher Woods; 77 London's Transport Museum; 78-81

Storstockholms Lokaltrafik AB, photos Hans Ekestang 79al, ar & b, 80b, 81a & b, Gerry Johansson 80a, Nils Ake Siversson 78; 82 WMTA, photo Paul Myatt; 83-85 WMTA, photo Larry Levine; 86-89 STIB, photo Peter Verbruggen; 90-93 Landeshauptstadt Munchen Baureferat; 94-98 Mark Thomas Photography; 100a Foster & Partners; 100b Foster & Partners, photo Aitor Ortiz; 101a & b Foster & Partners, photo Richard Davies; 102-3 Foster & Partners, photo Nigel Young; 104-106 Christopher Woods; 107, 108-9 Timothy Soar; 110-113 RATP, photos Bruno Margeurite 112, 113a, Jean François Mauboussin 110, 111, Bertrand Chabrol 113b; 114-117 Singapore MTR; 119-121 Toronto Transit Commission; 122a & b, 123 Hong Kong MTR; 124-127 Los Angeles County Metropolitan Transportation Authority, Creative Services, photos Tom Bonner; 128 Mark Thomas Photography; 130al Singapore MTR; 130ar WMATA, photo Larry Levine; 130b Singapore MTR; 131 all Sapporo Metro; 132-135 London's Transport Museum; 136 RATP; 137a, bl & r WMTA, photos Phil Portlock; 138, 139 © Martha Cooper; 140a STIB, photo Peter Verbruggen; 140b Capital Transport, 141 Mark Thomas Photography; 142 Capital Transport; 143a RATP, photo Giles Aligon; 143b RATP, photo Francois Mauboussin; 144l, c & r ICE; 145al Singapore MTR; 145ar Los Angeles County Metropolitan Transportation Authority, Creative Services, photo Tom Bonner; 145b KONE; 146 Christopher Woods; 147l & r Kristin Jarmund Architects, photo Jiri Havran; 148 Mark Ovenden; 149 Chicago Transit Authority; 150 RATP, photo Joel Thibaut; 151 RATP; 152a Mark Ovenden; 152b-153 London's Transport Museum, 154-55 Mark Ovenden; 157ar Mark Thomas Photography; 157bl, 158a ALSTOM; 158b Hong Kong MTR; 159a & b ALSTOM; 160a & b Alan Blake; 161 Toronto Transit Commission; 162l & r AS Oslo Sporveier; 163 AS Oslo Sporveier; 164 www.metro.ru; 165a Transporte Metropolitans de Barcelona; 165b Christopher Woods; 166 New York Metro; 167 Los Angeles County Metropolitan Transportation Authority, Creative Services, photo Tom Bonner.